Legends,
Sorcerers,
and Enchanted Lizards

The home of Modjie Samaké in the village of Senou, Djitoumou region (Cercle of Bamako) in 1969. The door and lock were sculpted in the nearby village of Zougoumé in 1896, and presented to her by her parents at the time of her marriage to Tyéblé Coulibaly.

Legends, Sorcerers, and Enchanted Lizards

DOOR LOCKS OF THE BAMANA OF MALI

Pascal James Imperato

AFRICANA PUBLISHING COMPANY
New York and London

This publication accompanies an exhibition held at The African Art Museum of the S.M.A. Fathers in Tenafly, New Jersey opening October 2001.

Published in the United States of America 2001
by Africana Publishing Company,
an imprint of Holmes & Meier Publishers, Inc.
160 Broadway • New York, NY 10038
www.holmesandmeier.com

This publication is funded in part by the New Jersey State Council on the Arts, Department of State, through grant funds administered by the Bergen County Department of Parks, Division of Cultural and Historic Affairs.

Designed by Brigid McCarthy

Library of Congress Cataloging-in-Publication Data

Imperato, Pascal James.
    Legends, sorcerers, and enchanted lizards : door locks of the Bamana of Mali / Pascal James Imperato.
        p.cm.
    Includes bibliographical references.
        ISBN 0-8419-1416-8 (cloth : alk. paper)—ISBN 0-8419-1414-1 (paper : alk. paper)
        1. Bambara (Bamana : African people)—Material culture—Exhibitions. 2. Wooden locks—Mali—Exhibitions. 3. Sculpture, Bambara—Exhibitions. 4. Bambara (African people)—Religion—Exhibitions. I. Title.

DT551.45.B35 I46 2001
683'.32'096623—dc21   2001024169

Manufactured in the United States of America

Dedicated with gratitude to my Malian friends and colleagues,
without whom this volume would not have been possible,
and to Paule Brasseur, the late Gérard Brasseur, and the late Dominique Zahan,
who greatly encouraged me in my research studies in Mali

Contents

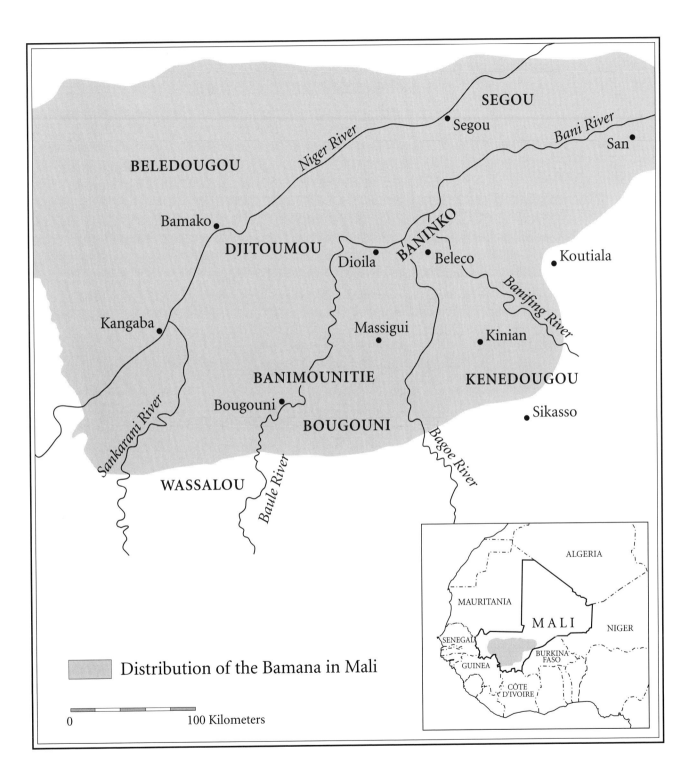

BELEDOUGOU

SEGOU

Segou

Niger River

Bani River

San

Bamako

DJITOUMOU

BANINKO

Dioila

Beleco

Koutiala

Kangaba

Massigui

Kinian

Banifing River

BANIMOUNITIE

KENEDOUGOU

Sankarani River

Bougouni

Sikasso

BOUGOUNI

Bagoe River

WASSALOU

Baule River

Distribution of the Bamana in Mali

0   100 Kilometers

ALGERIA

MAURITANIA

MALI

SENEGAL

NIGER

GUINEA

BURKINA FASO

CÔTE D'IVOIRE

Principal traditional regions of the Bamana country in Mali.

Foreword

IT IS ESPECIALLY GRATIFYING for the African Art Museum of the S.M.A. Fathers to present the exhibition *Legends, Sorcerers, and Enchanted Lizards. Door Locks of the Bamana of Mali*, and this publication that accompanies it. The Bamana of Mali are well known for their rich art traditions which include masks, statues, antelope headdresses, puppets, iron sculptures, and door locks. Among all the peoples of West Africa who sculpt wooden door locks, including the Bwa, Dogon, Lobi, Mossi, and Senufo, the Bamana have created the greatest variety, intimately linked to their legends and mythico-religious ethos.

The objects presented in this exhibition and its accompanying publication are all from the collection of Dr. Pascal James and Eleanor M. Imperato. This collection and the exhibition are unique from several perspectives. Dr. Imperato, a leading authority on the Bamana and their art, as well as an internationally respected scholar of Mali, assembled this collection in the field over three decades ago. At that time, he began his field studies of the Bamana, Dogon, and Peul of Mali, covering art, history, anthropology, and traditional medicine. He became a pioneer American scholar who, in Mali's early years of independence, studied and described the material culture of the Bamana from both an anthropological and an art history perspective. His early publications such as The Dance of the Tyi Wara (*African Arts*, 1970), and Last Dances of the Bambara (*Natural History*, 1975) placed the art of the Bamana within broader social and spiritual contexts, and helped make it accessible to a large English-speaking public. His in-depth studies of specific Bamana and Dogon art traditions also gave access to the public through such publications as *Dogon Cliff Dwellers. The Art of Mali's Mountain People* (1978), and *Buffoons, Queens and Wooden Horsemen. The Dyo and Gouan Societies of the Bambara of Mali* (1983).

The breadth of Dr. Imperato's field studies also enabled him to interpret Bamana art against the broader canvas of Mali's rich historical, social, and cultural traditions, well documented in his other works such as *Mali. A Search for Direction* (1989), and *Historical Dictionary of Mali* (1977, 1986, 1996).

His initial five-year stay in Mali, followed by return visits and ongoing field research with Malian collaborators, has enabled him to obtain unique insights into Bamana art traditions over a span of thirty-five years. This publication is greatly enriched by his ongoing scholarly endeavors.

Dr. Imperato was able to conduct his initial field studies of the Bamana and their art in widely diverse geographic locations because of the essential character of his mission to Mali, which was to eradicate smallpox, control measles, and immunize the entire population of the country against cholera, meningococcal meningitis, and yellow fever. A public health physician and specialist in tropical medicine, his training as an epidemiologist at the U.S. Centers for Disease Control and Prevention, and his previous experience as a medical anthropologist in Tanzania, enabled him to apply the meticulous methodologies of scientific inquiry and evidence gathering to the study of Bamana art traditions. As a result, his careful inquiries were conducted over a wide geographic area, and based on data gathered from many informants. Inherent in all of his studies, including those of locks, is the vital scientific principle of corroboration of evidence and documentation of differences in evidence secured in distant locales from those who were strangers to one another. This approach, coupled with the temporal span of his studies over three-and-a-half decades, has enabled him to document not only commonalities and differences in beliefs and traditions from one place to another, but also temporal changes resulting from both internal and external influences on Bamana society.

Bamana locks are regularly presented in museum and gallery exhibitions, and have occasionally been shown as either a distinct group (*Porte & Serrature Dogon & Bambara. Selezionate da: Denise e Beppe Berna*, 1980), or as part of collections of other locks (Rodriques, Georges D. *A Collection of West African Doors and Locks*, 1968; West African Door Locks. An Exhibition of Tribal Arts Gallery Two, *African Arts*, 1974). However, *Legends, Sorcerers, and Enchanted Lizards* is unique in that no previous exhibition or publication can equal the range and quality of the objects shown nor the meticulous fieldwork-based scholarship that underlies the description of every lock or door exhibited. In addition, all the objects presented are documented as to geographic provenance, and, with the exception of one, were all collected in the field by a highly respected scholar whose information about them derives from knowledgeable Bamana collaborators.

This publication is divided into three sections. The first two, "The Bamana World" and "Portals, Doors, and Locks," are enriched by exceptional field photographs and extensive references. They offer readers a vivid overview of the Bamana, their way of life, their legendary and religious beliefs, and the meanings and roles of doors and locks in their daily lives. Detailed captions accompany all sculptures illustrated in the third "Catalogue" section, and greatly assist readers in arriving at an understanding of their meanings within the context of Bamana beliefs. An especially unique feature is that the sculptor-blacksmiths who created three of the locks are known, and were close collaborators of the author. As a result of all these exceptional features, *Legends, Sorcerers, and Enchanted Lizards* is a landmark publication on Bamana art, and contributes immeasurably to our knowledge of these remarkable people and their art traditions. The museum is indeed proud to present this exhibition, and grateful to Pascal James Imperato and Eleanor M. Imperato for offering the public an opportunity to view their collection.

We are grateful to Professor Patrick R. McNaughton of Indiana University, a leading Bamana scholar, for his beautiful and authoritative introduction to this volume. Special thanks are extended to Miriam Holmes, Publisher, and Maggie Kennedy, Executive Editor, Holmes & Meier Publishers, for their enthusiastic support of this volume. We also wish to thank Brigid McCarthy, who beautifully designed this book and oversaw its production. The publication of this book was made possible in part by the New Jersey State Council on the Arts, Department of State, through grant funds administered by the Bergen County Department of Parks, Division of Cultural and Historic Affairs, for which we are extremely grateful.

Legends, Sorcerers, and Enchanted Lizards represents the latest of a series of exhibitions presented by the African Art Museum of the S.M.A. Fathers. In 1996, we presented *The Artistry of Traditional Sculpture*, curated by Charles Bordogna; in 1997, *Nigerian Art from the Collection of Judith and*

Leonard Kahan; and that same year, *Keepers of the History. African Art from the Collection of Dr. Michael Berger*, which was accompanied by an essay authored by Donna Page. Planned future exhibitions include *Songye Kifwebe Masks from the Collection of Stewart J. Warkow*, to be curated by Marc Leo Felix; *Sculpture of East Africa from the Collection of Carl and Wilma Zabel*; and *Father Kevin Carroll, S.M.A.*, which will be drawn from our own holdings and other public and private collections. This last-named exhibition, honoring an exceptionally dedicated S.M.A. Father who made important contributions to our knowledge of African art, will be organized in association with the Irish Province of the S.M.A. Fathers, and mounted at both our museum in Tenafly, New Jersey, and at a new exhibition facility at Dromantine, Newry, County Down, Ireland. Exhibitions such as these enable us to provide public access to exceptional collections of African Art.

The African Art Museum of the S.M.A. Fathers, founded almost forty years ago, has formed representative collections of the traditional arts of sub-Saharan Africa. In the 1960s, objects of ethnological and artistic interest were acquired through purchase from the S.M.A. museums at Lyon, France, and Cadier en Keer, Netherlands, and other vendors, and through donation of pieces collected in Africa by S.M.A. Fathers on missionary assignment there. In the past twenty years, the collections have been greatly augmented by annual donations from many generous private collectors. Key in this development has been Charles Bordogna, who served as volunteer curator for many years, and Leonard Kahan, former president of L. Kahan Gallery/African Arts, New York City, who brought the African Art Museum to the attention of his many colleagues in the field. In the last few years, the small but dedicated staff of the museum that includes Audrey Koenig, Registrar; Pamela Smith, Textile Conservator; Boniface Kiamue, Consultant on Computer Technology; and Thomas Shannon, Exhibition Designer, has ably assisted me in the documentation, care, and presentation of the collections. Our goal is to have relatively comprehensive but excellent and manageable collections. Our efforts to reach that goal have been aided by the connoisseurship of experts such as Irwin Hersey, Harmer Johnson, Leonard Kahan, Dr. Henry John Drewal, Marc Leo Felix, William Wright, and Charles Bordogna, each of whom has reviewed all or parts of the museum's collections. The guidance of the members of the museum's Acquisitions Committee has been of the greatest value. It is comprised of Irwin Hersey, Chair, Dr. Michael Berger, Dr. Noble Endicott, Dr. Pascal James Imperato, Dr. Marshall W. Mount, Stewart J. Warkow, and Carl Zabel.

Without the concerned and sympathetic support of the Council of the American Province of the Society of African Missions; Reverend Ulick Bourke, S.M.A. Provincial Superior; Reverend Brendan Darcy, S.M.A. Vice Provincial and Local Superior; Reverend Clark Yates, Secretary; and Reverend James C. Hickey, Treasurer, the work of the museum could not go forward in an ordered and meaningful way. To the Council, the S.M.A. Fathers of the American Province, and the staff at the Mission, I express warm and sincere gratitude for their continuing and unfailing interest and spirit of cooperation, all of which have made exhibitions such as *Legends, Sorcerers, and Enchanted Lizards* possible.

Robert J. Koenig
Director
The African Art Museum of the S.M.A. Fathers

Preface and Acknowledgments

IN EARLY 1967, I traveled south from Mali's capital, Bamako, to the Bamana village of Kéléya in order to investigate and control a measles epidemic. I had arrived in Mali in late 1966 to direct a smallpox eradication and measles control program sponsored by the United States Agency for International Development, and the United States Public Health Service. This was my first visit to a rural Bamana village.

While examining and treating a group of children inside the village, I happened to glance to my left. There I saw a remarkable sculpted object standing in relief on the surface of a house door. It was dark in color, had a stylized human face, and what appeared to be two horns protruding from its head. A horizontal bar ran behind its back. This object looked straight ahead, standing like a sentinel prepared to protect the house and those who lived within. Its iconography expressed enormous power tinged with threat, and I found myself somewhat hesitant to approach it. My response to this object was precisely what its creator had intended. However, I could not have known this at the time since my knowledge of the Bamana, their philosophical and religious beliefs, and their way of life, was extremely rudimentary.

At first, I thought that this object was sculpted in relief on the left-sided plank of the door, but my assistant, Djigui Diakité, told me that it was a *konbarabara* (door lock) attached with nails to the door. Seeing the woman who lived in the house, he asked if I could examine the lock, and she readily agreed. This was the first Bamana lock I had ever seen, and I was absolutely amazed by the mechanics of the locking system that lay hidden within its exquisite exterior. I did not know then that Kéléya was famous as a center of door-lock sculpting or that traditional Bamana religious and philosophical beliefs were still vibrant in this part of Mali. The beautiful lock that I saw and touched that day in Kéléya stimulated my interest in these beliefs and in the sculptures through which the Bamana express them.

I lived and worked in Mali for five subsequent years following this experience, and returned several times for extensive stays. My role in assisting the Malians in investigating and controlling epidemics of smallpox, measles, yellow fever, cholera and meningococcal meningitis, and in vaccinating the population against these diseases, enabled me to travel throughout the country with several mobile teams of nurses and vaccinators. During my long stays in rural Bamana villages, I was able to pursue my studies of their many art forms, including door locks. Even then, there was an open frontier between these rural areas and Bamako, Mali's capital, which had a modest population of only 250,000. Bamako's *quartiers* of that time shared many characteristics with rural villages, and the presence in them of recent immigrants from those villages permitted further inquiries.

During the first two years of my work in Mali, the country was governed by an anti-American Marxist dictatorship headed by President Modibo Keita. Americans attached to the United States Embassy were not permitted to travel outside the Cercle of Bamako without submitting a written request five working days before departure. The requests were frequently denied. Such travel restrictions would have made it impossible for me to effectively function as a public health physician. After strong protests from the United States Embassy, the Malians relented and allowed me to travel unhindered. The presence of representatives of the ruling political party, the *Union Soudanaise-Rassemblement Démocratique Africain,* and daily anti-American diatribes on Radio Mali in French and other national languages created significant problems for me in towns and administrative centers. However, I was always well received in rural villages whose peasant farmers strongly resented the Marxist regime's agrarian policies. These included continuous attempts to collectivize agriculture and purchase grain below fair market value in order to keep retail prices artificially low in Bamako.

The government of Modibo Keita actively discouraged Westerners from learning and speaking *Bamanan-kan* and other indigenous languages. It also denied permission to most Western scholars who wished to conduct field research in Mali. These policies emanated not only from the repressive police-state character of the government, but also out of concerns that language fluency and travel in rural areas could give access to information about popular discontent with existing policies and programs.

Hostility toward Americans was especially evident in Bamako, fueled in part by the government's desire to please its Communist patrons. In Bamako, many Malians even refused to reply to my greeting them in *Bamanan-kan.* One of my Malian colleagues cautioned me that my speaking the language in Bamako would intensify suspicions that I was an intelligence agent. By contrast, people in rural villages were pleased that a foreigner was attempting to speak their language, and conversed freely with me.

There were no formal courses in *Bamanan-kan* available to Americans in Mali at the time. However, both Protestant and Catholic missionaries had published dictionaries, grammars, and self-study guides. I was fortunate in being able to obtain these from the Reverend Edward Tschetter and the Reverend Earl Gripp of the Gospel Missionary Union, and the Reverend Franz Van der Weijst of the Roman Catholic Archdiocese of Bamako. In time, some of my Malian colleagues helped me to study the language. Following the 1968 military coup d'etat that ousted Modibo Keita and his government, people in general were more willing to converse with Westerners in *Bamanan-kan.*

The information presented in this volume on Bamana door locks represents the knowledge of many people. My role has been to transmit it in a synthesized and interpreted manner understandable to Westerners, and to place it against the broader canvas of the beliefs and way of life of the Bamana people. This knowledge was drawn from diverse areas of the Bamana country, and thus provides broad perspectives with regard to beliefs and interpretations of symbolism.

This volume is divided into three broad sections. The first, "The Bamana World," provides an overview of the Bamana and their philosophical and spiritual beliefs. Included in it is a detailed discussion of graphic signs and their meanings. The second section, "Portals, Doors, and Locks," presents detailed discussions of Bamana doors and locks, and related topics. Each of these sections is provided with extensive references and illustrations which supplement the information presented in the text. The captions to the photographs in these two sections contain additional information, and often identify objects and scenes by village, traditional region, and modern administrative unit (cercle). Although the latter two may have identical names (e.g., Segou), traditional regions usually include more than one modern cercle. The "Catalogue" which is divided into eight sub-sections, contains extensive captions on each of the seventy-one objects illustrated. Among these are fifty-five Bamana locks, four Bamana doors with locks, ten Dogon locks, and two Bwa locks. The Dogon and Bwa locks are shown for comparative purposes.

The "Catalogue" section captions compliment the information contained in the two previous sections of the volume. These captions give detailed information about the symbolic meanings of various forms, interpretations of graphic signs, and descriptions of locking devices. The provenance of each Bamana lock is given first by modern administrative unit (cercle) and then by traditional Bamana region in parentheses. In addition, the Bamana locks have been grouped into five thematic sections in order to facilitate reader understanding of symbolic meanings. However, a fuller comprehension of the meanings of a given lock and its graphic signs requires a reading of the first two sections of this volume.

At the time of my early field studies, there was still a large number of door locks in place in villages, as well as elders and sculptor-blacksmiths who were familiar with their meanings. To understand what they had to say about these locks required that I study thoroughly the published works of the pioneer French scholars, Solange de Ganay, Maurice Delafosse, Germaine Dieterlen, Joseph Henry, Henri Labouret, Charles Monteil, Viviana Paques, Louis Tauxier, and Dominique Zahan, and the writings of the pioneer Malian ethnographers, Moussa Travélé and Youssouf Cissé. Only after so doing was I able to converse with Bamana elders and sculptor-blacksmiths from a position of commonly shared knowledge.

I acquired the locks presented in this volume in Mali during the years I lived there (1966–1971). Many are architectonically identical or similar to others I studied in situ in rural villages, and possess pyroengraved surface graphic signs that I also saw in the field. Thus, it was possible to record with great certainty their overall symbolic meanings based on information I obtained from elders and sculptor-blacksmiths. Some locks depicted here, however, possess architectonics I did not see in any that were still in situ in villages. However, I was able to show these locks to informants in the areas from where they came, and in so doing establish their symbolic meanings. The sculptor-blacksmiths who sculpted three of the Bamana locks illustrated are known, as are the people for whom they were made (Figures 15, 43, and 44). I was able to work closely with these blacksmiths, and thus obtain clear insights into the symbolic messages they intended their locks to convey. While these objects represent only a small proportion of the fifty-nine Bamana sculptures illustrated, the information about them is significant for an art tradition where anonymity of authorship is usually the rule. Of the four Bamana doors illustrated, the family of blacksmiths that created one is known, as are the village provenances for all four.

The field research on which this study is principally based was conducted in Mali between 1966 and 1975. I conducted additional research during the 1980s and 1990s. Improved telephonic, facsimile, and e-mail services in Mali in the past decade greatly facilitated communications with my research assistants and informants. They were able to clarify points of ambiguity and provide needed details as I began the long process of synthesizing my earlier field notes. One of my assistants, Amadou Sanogo, was able to interview sculptor-blacksmiths in rural areas of the Cercle of Segou, and communicate his findings to me by e-mail or facsimile a few days later. Similarly, Modibo N'Faly Keita, who traveled with me throughout most of Mali, conducted additional field research for me in the Djitoumou area, and communicated his findings to me by telephone. I found that modern communication technologies could serve as a unique bridge between researcher and assistant, since both were familiar with the larger corpus of information previously collected together in the field.

My field studies were conducted throughout the Bamana country in Baninko, Banimounitie, Bélédougou, Bougouni, Djitoumou, Kénédougou, and Segou. I also carried out observations in Malinké villages in the Fouladougou Arbala, Fouladougou Saboula, and Birgo. Throughout these studies, I was greatly aided and guided by the late Djigui Diakité, Modibo N'Faly Keita, Amadou Sanogo, Lassana Traoré, and by the many nurses, vaccinators, and health personnel with whom I traveled and who greatly facilitated my contacts in regions from where they came. Among these, I want to especially thank Amadou Coulibaly, Kelicouma Konaté, Dramane Samaké, Kassim Sangaré, and Moulaye Traoré.

The late renowned Malian bard (*dyeli*), Batrou Sekou Kouyaté, not only taught me to play the *kora*, but also to interpret some of the legends depicted in certain locks. Kolékélé Mariko, Moussa Traoré, and N'Tyi Traoré helped me to understand the symbolism of some locks from Baninko and Bougouni. The late Modjie Samaké of the village of Senou provided unique details about her house door and lock which are illustrated as they were in situ in 1969. Her grandson, Aliou Coulibaly, a former *ton tigui* (*ton* leader) and current *dougou tigui* (village leader) of Senou, was of great assistance to me in my studies from 1968 through 2000.

I am especially grateful to several remarkable Bamana master-sculptor blacksmiths who were great repositories of theological and philosophical knowledge in addition to being highly accomplished artists and craftsmen. They were patient teachers from whom I learned much of what I now know about Bamana door locks. All of them are now deceased, and I sincerely regret that they did not see this project brought to fruition. Among them were: Moussa Coulibaly (Touganabougou), Makan Fané (Niossombougou), Siriman Fané (Koké), Bafing Kané (Koké), and Karamoko Kanté (Ngoloba).

Abdoulaye Sylla of the Musée Nationale in Bamako has greatly assisted me over the past three decades. I am very grateful to him for generously helping me to interpret the symbolism of certain paradigms depicted in locks, and for sharing with me his profound knowledge of the Bamana and their traditional religious and philosophical beliefs. I also wish to thank Yaya Diallo, co-author of *The Healing Drum*, who graciously shared his knowledge of *Bamanaya* among the Minianka.

The late Dominique Zahan, one of the great pioneer researchers among the Bamana, encouraged me in my studies, offered guidance, and enthusiastically shared his vast knowledge of the Bamana. Paule Brasseur and the late Gérard Brasseur also encouraged and assisted me in my research over many years.

This exhibition and publication have been in preparation for five years. Many individuals contributed to making them possible. Robert J. Koenig, Director of the African Art Museum of the S.M.A. Fathers, has been a guiding hand behind this exhibition and publication, and untiring in his efforts to make them a reality. I am personally grateful to him for his steadfast support. I want to express my thanks to the Reverend Ulick Bourke, S.M.A., Provincial Superior of the American Province of the Society of African Missions, and President of the Board of Trustees of the African Art Museum, and to the Reverend Brendan Darcy, S.M.A., Vice-Provincial and Local Superior, Vice-President of the Board of Trustees of the African Art Museum, and Local Superior of the Society of African Missions, Tenafly, New Jersey, for hosting this exhibition and for being enthusiastic supporters of it.

During the years I lived and worked in Mali, I collected over a hundred Bamana and forty Dogon locks. Of these, fifty-five Bamana locks were chosen for the exhibition and for illustration in the catalogue section of this volume. Four Bamana doors with locks, which I also collected, were chosen, as well as ten of the forty Dogon locks. In addition, the two Bwa locks I brought from Mali are also included. The selection of objects was a difficult task, guided by a need to present as broad a range of sculptural, thematic, and regional diversity as possible. I am very grateful to Leonard Kahan, who directed the choice of objects, and who provided valuable assistance and advice on many aspects of the exhibition and publication. I also want to thank him for first suggesting this exhibition, and for being a constant supporter of it. I am grateful to Donna Page, who expertly mounted all of the locks, and provided valuable advice about the exhibition and publication.

Unless otherwise noted, the field photographs were taken by me during the course of my research. I want to thank Marli Shamir of Jerusalem, Israel, for granting me permission to use a number of her beautiful photographs. I also wish to thank Christraud Geary, Curator, and Anita Jenkins, Archives Technician, the Eliot Elisofon Photographic Archives of the National Museum of African Art, Smithsonian Institution, for providing a photograph that the late Eliot Elisofon took of one of my locks during one of his visits to Mali in 1970.

Chris Lopez expertly photographed all of the locks and doors illustrated in the Catalogue section of this volume. I appreciate the care she took to capture the beauty and surface details of these objects. I want to thank John Schaub for printing many of the photographs, and Chris Brest for drawing the map, graphic signs, and door. Janet Stanley, Director of the Warren M. Robbins Library of the National Museum of Art, Smithsonian Institution, provided me with copies of numerous publications over the years, for which I am thankful. Miriam Holmes, Publisher, and Maggie Kennedy, Executive Editor, Holmes & Meier Publishers, provided enthusiasm, suggestions, and guidance; and Brigid McCarthy designed and expertly supervised this volume's production. Katharine Turok, former Executive Editor, Holmes & Meier Publishers, gave valuable advice concerning the publication of this book. I am very grateful to Lois Hahn who patiently and expertly prepared numerous drafts of the manuscript and made many helpful suggestions about revisions.

I want to especially thank Professor Patrick R. McNaughton of Indiana University for writing the Introduction, and for his advice and helpful suggestions.

My wife, Eleanor, read several drafts of the manuscript, and made important editorial suggestions. I am very grateful to her and to our children, Alison, Gavin, and Austin, for their help with various aspects of this exhibition.

This publication is funded in part by the New Jersey State Council on the Arts, Department of State, through grant funds administered by the Bergen County Department of Parks, Division of Cultural and Historic Affairs. We are most grateful for this generous support.

PASCAL JAMES IMPERATO

Introduction: Unlocking the Door to a Rich and Wonderful World

THE DOOR LOCKS USED BY THE BAMANA, and many other peoples in West Africa, should be considered wonderful artistic accomplishments. When viewed from a distance in the small towns of Mali, it is as if sculpted animals or characters from a story were stuck to the doors of people's homes. They are not exactly where a door knob would be in an American home, but the horizontal element that disappears into the earthen door jamb suggests even to foreigners that this may be some sort of locking mechanism. But what a locking mechanism!

In 1971, I went to Mali for the first time, a graduate student doing art history research. It was Pat Imperato who picked me up at the airport and took me to my hotel. As I began my research, one of the first interesting encounters I had involved a door lock. I knew very little about these locks, but I was seeing them everywhere. Something I found particularly interesting was that the metal keys were often left in them while people were off in the fields farming or otherwise away from their homes.

One day, I asked a woman about this, and, in a confident tone, she told me to try to open her lock with the key. I tried and tried, and after about five minutes gave up. I was wiggling the key around in the lock in every way I could think of, and I just could not get its iron prongs to find the iron pegs and push them up out of the holes that held the mechanism in its locked position. This was viewed as hilarious by the ten or so people who were watching. It got even funnier when the woman challenged her husband to try to open that lock, and, key in hand, he could not do it either.

These locks are highly personal. They have their own peculiarities and personalities, which are wonderfully intertwined with the lives of the people who own them. They are often made by excellent artists, and possess great formal subtlety. People charge their imagery with important social and spiritual meanings. In short, they are eminently worthy of the full-length treatment that Pat Imperato gives them, and in the pages that follow you will see that he has served them well.

You hold in your hands an excellent book, by a person very qualified to write it. Africa has long been a catalyst for the imaginations of people in the Western world, as well as a resource for many of the West's most shamefully acquired gains. But Africa is also a wellspring of ideas about the world, ideas from which everyone can benefit. And it is a source of visual and verbal arts with refined articulations that promote contemplation and applaud the vitality of human imagination. The door locks this book presents are perfect examples, and, thanks to the author, you have the opportunity to consider them thoroughly and sensitively.

The information and illustrations that follow are a doorway to a complex, refined, and sophisticated African world of art. You can enjoy the beauty of these door locks. You can appreciate the creativity embedded in their designs and imagery. You can think about the world of ideas and activities of which they are a part. You can contemplate the human condition, with all of its associated issues and problems, through the locks' symbols and motifs. And you can consider and perhaps even be influenced by some of the strategies Bamana people use to live in the world, as expressed through *Bamanaya* (the ideas and practices of Bamana culture) manifest in these locks. One of the important things art does is fuel the imagination with the ideas and values, sentiments, and perspectives of other people. Often this gives you the opportunity to measure and expand your own understanding of the world and consider with fresh eyes your place in it. This book is rich enough to offer all that.

The door locks of West Africa's savannah lands are an impressive artistic tradition. They are utterly utilitarian as ingenious mechanisms to lock doors. But they are also highly artistic, composed according to sophisticated aesthetics with embellishment and imagery that range from quietly elegant to provocatively forceful. And they are deeply evocative of the meanings and values that Bamana people use to live their lives. They are loaded with symbolic references to ideas and beliefs about people, society, and the spiritual, indirectly through a body of animal and mythical characters. Thus the locks are conceptually complex, and they defy Western categorization. Are they art or craft? Are they sacred or secular? They are all of these, and they are more. Because often, too, these locks are presented as gifts to newly married individuals, and as they age with the marriage, they serve as a beloved marker for an individual or a family group's personal history. These locks can be highly cherished possessions, and they are important components in a much larger tradition of fine arts.

Pat Imperato focuses primarily on door locks made and used by the Bamana people, who are linguistically and historically part of a very large West African culture called *Mande*. Mande people have become known the world over for their ancient trade networks and enormous empires. They have also become famous for their visual and oral arts. The first public exhibition of Bamana art in America was organized by Robert Goldwater in 1960, at the Museum of Primitive Art in New York (many of the objects in that show are now at the Metropolitan Museum of Art).[1] At that time, outside of West Africa, the only information available on Bamana art resided in the accounts of explorers, colonial officials, missionaries, and an emerging group of French anthropologists headed by Marcel Griaule (whose work did not focus on art, but did contain much of relevance). Information was not always easy to find, but Goldwater did an excellent job of assembling and presenting it.

Just six years later, Pat Imperato began the work in Mali that would ultimately lead to this book. Africa was not new to him. He had already worked as a doctor in East Africa, and, in fact, had already written a book about his experiences.[2] But only a very capable and adventurous person would have accepted the job in Mali. The goal was the eradication of smallpox and the control of measles through inoculation—in a country whose infrastructure of roads and services were under severe post-colonial duress, whose population included huge numbers of highly mobile nomads, whose terrain included an enormous amount of the Sahara Desert, and whose government was Marxist and not the least bit friendly or accommodating to Americans. But a better person could not have been found.

Pat Imperato, with a team of dedicated Malian professionals, did eradicate smallpox and control measles in Mali. And during that time, he developed a strong admiration for Mande and Bamana culture. With a good doctor's penchant for observing and recording fine detail with an open mind, he, at the end of his five years in Mali, knew more about Bamana society, culture, and art than many scholars. He proved to be an outstanding ethnographer, and the fruits of his research began to emerge shortly after he returned to the states.

Pat was one of the featured participants in the first international symposium on Mande studies, held in London in 1972. Since then, he has published a lengthy string of articles and books that present Bamana visual arts in deep, rich, and exciting detail. He has written on antelope headdresses, young men's masquerades, door locks, cloth, monumental figural sculpture, small twin figures, the arts of the spiritual associations, and traditional medical practices.[3] He even wrote a memoir of his experiences in Mali, and that book demonstrates the kind of person Pat is.[4] The information you are about to read comes from a perceptive, sensitive, and intelligent individual, who enjoyed and respected the society he found himself in, and who has long contributed to the rest of the world's better understanding of it. Mande people believe in the power of travel for the sake of gaining knowledge and experience in the world. They also believe in the importance of a strong work ethic. Herein you will find the fruits of those things.

For the academic community, this book is significant. First, it is the only extensive publication devoted to door locks. The subject matter of African art history is far more vast than the publications on it, and it is unfortunately uncommon for many worthy art traditions to receive in-depth coverage. Thus, a detailed work of scholarship such as this is most welcome.

Next, the author takes a holistic approach to writing about Bamana art. He encourages you to ask: Where does the art stop and other social or cultural phenomena start? His answer is that it is very hard to determine, and far better to extend the discussion into culture than to constrict it snugly around the art.

You might think of an artwork as a point in conceptual space. But it is stuck like glue to an almost endless array of ideas, activities, and experiences that everyone in that culture who views it invokes. A good percentage of what is invoked will be rather personal, and so scholars cannot generalize about it. But a very good percentage of it will also belong to beliefs and practices that people have in common. They may discuss them frequently, argue about them, and disagree on the finer points of their meaning and significance. But they do so on the common ground that scholars can indeed generalize about.

The particular value of this book is that it presents a large swath of that common ground. You might think this is more information than you need to appreciate the locks. You are right; you can simply admire their shapes and designs. But Pat takes you to a point where you can understand how Bamana people appreciate them, because you can see the kinds of associations they have to ideas about people, families, social life, and the spiritual realm. This cannot help but make your appreciation a great deal richer, and that is what good art history and ethnography should do.

Pat's thick-information approach also helps us see the value of art as more than entertainment, something that Americans often fail to recognize. Somehow many of us have come to consider art as strictly entertainment, a spare time enterprise that emphasizes pleasure and the senses. But, in fact, art can be (and often is) an important component of thought for people considering who they are and how they are doing. The contextual materials Pat presents for these locks demonstrate that they are charged with that kind of potential. In one sense, a door lock is a simple thing, a single embellished image stuck on a door. But you can see from this book that a door lock is also far more, and that can lead you to the realization that art can be conceptually complicated and related to many realms of human thought and activity.

A related contribution emerges here too. Just as Americans often see art as belonging to the domain of pleasurable pastimes, they also often see it as a passive part of society, or as merely reflecting ideas that are enacted more seriously in other arenas. But that is not always the case. In fact, very often in every society, art is proactive, even if everyone does not realize it. Art presents and promotes ideas and activities. It empowers people. It is an instrument in the maneuverings and negotiations that compose people's lives, and this book demonstrates that.

Pat also indirectly makes an important contribution to a debate in the field of Mande studies. The French school of anthropology, headed by Marcel Griaule, has long been a source of controversy for Mande scholars. Many people have asserted that information from that group is often the product of preconceived ideas, leading questions asked during research, and poor translations of information people provided in their own language (*Bamanan-kan*).[5] A major criticism is that these scholars have been too preoccupied with myth, and have made far too strong an argument for its manifestations in daily life. Another is that they have created a view of Mande culture that is too organized and systematic to reflect the realities of Mande people's actual lives. These are serious criticisms and have been the subject of several serious scholarly publications.

As Pat began to understand Mande society and culture, in the midst of his personal experiences in Mali, he was unfamiliar with the work of this body of French research. He only delved into it thoroughly upon his return to America. And then he read it carefully and systematically. He found that much of what he read was corroborated from his own personal experiences.

We know that Griaule and his colleagues gave myth an enormously prominent place in their research. We know, too, that they made vast generalizations about what people believe that did not take into account the tremendous variations that come from people's personal histories and interests. But a great many of their findings are, in fact, highly useful, and Pat's work helps to demonstrate that.

This book is divided into three major sections, which take you by degrees into the world of Bamana door locks. If you are anxious to begin appreciating the formal qualities of these creations, skip right away to the catalogue entries. But when you are ready to explore the world of ideas and activities that give these locks their value in Bamana society, go back to the beginning. In the section "The Bamana World," you will encounter the general tenets that Bamana use to explain themselves and their universe. In the section "Portals, Doors, and Locks," you will discover an extensive collection of Bamana ideas about the nature of people and the need for locks. You will also get a glimpse of the history of these locks, and a closer look at the artists who made them.

I have enjoyed Bamana door locks for over thirty years. It is a tribute to The African Art Museum of the S.M.A. Fathers that they saw the value of doing such an exhibition, and making this book possible. I, for one, am deeply appreciative. The exhibition is a significant contribution to the study of African art, and so is this fine book.

PATRICK R. MCNAUGHTON
Professor of African Art
Department of Art History
Indiana University

REFERENCES

1. Goldwater, Robert. *Bambara Sculpture from the Western Sudan.* New York: University Publishers, Inc., 1960.

2. Imperato, Pascal James. *Bwana Doctor.* London: Jarrolds Publishers Ltd., 1967.

3. See Imperato, Pascal James. The Dance of the Tyi Wara. *African Arts* 1970; IV(1):8–13, 71–80; Contemporary Masked Dances and Masquerades of the Bamana (Bambara) Age Sets from the Cercle of Bamako. Paper presented at the Conference on Manding Studies/Congrès d'Etudes Manding. London: University of London, School of Oriental and African Studies, 1972; *The Cultural Heritage of Africa.* Chanute, Kansas: Safari Museum Press, 1974; *Historical Dictionary of Mali.* Third Edition. Lanham, Maryland: The Scarecrow Press, Inc., 1996; *African Folk Medicine. Practices and Beliefs of the Bambara and Other Peoples.* Baltimore: York Press, 1977; Bambara and Malinke Ton Masquerades. *African Arts* 1980; XIII(4):47–55, 82–85, 87; and *Buffoons, Queens and Wooden Horsemen. The Dyo and Gouan Societies of the Bambara of Mali.* New York: Kilima House Publishers, 1983.

4. Imperato, Pascal James. *A Wind in Africa. A Story of Modern Medicine in Mali.* St. Louis: Warren H. Green, Inc., 1975.

5. See Calame-Griaule, Geneviève. On the Dogon Revisited. *Current Anthropology* 1991; 32(5):575–577; Clifford, James. Power and Dialogue in Ethnography: Marcel Griaule's Initiation. In *Observers Observed: Essays on Ethnographic Fieldwork* by George W. Stocking, Jr. (editor). Madison: University of Wisconsin Press, 1983, 121–156; and Van Beek, Walter E.A. Dogon Restudied. A Field Evaluation of the Work of Marcel Griaule. *Current Anthropology* 1991; 32(4):139–167.

Legends,
Sorcerers,
and Enchanted Lizards

THE BAMANA WORLD

THE BAMANA (BAMBARA), comprising some three-and-a-half million people, are the largest ethnic group in Mali. They are agriculturalists who primarily live in an inverted triangular area in west central Mali covering 400,000 square miles of flat savanna and sahel. Smaller groups of Bamana, descendants of migrants of previous centuries, live beyond the confines of this area, especially to the northeast in the Niger Bend. The Bamana occupy a dominant political, social, and economic position in modern Mali, and their language, *Bamanan-kan*, is the lingua franca in much of the country. The Bamana belong to the Mande family of peoples, which also includes the Malinké (Maninka) and the Dyula. The former live to the west of the Bamana in Mali, Guinea, and Senegal, while the latter are found primarily in the Ivory Coast.[1]

BAMANA SOCIETY

Although the Bamana are primarily agriculturists, cultivating millet, corn, and manioc, many keep sizeable herds of cattle, sheep, and goats. They live in villages that vary in population from 100 or so to over 1,000, the average village in the early twenty-first century having about 500 inhabitants. They are polygamous, patriarchal, patrilineal, and patrilocal. Marriage involves a bride price paid to the woman's parents, and consists of livestock, clothing, textiles, and in recent years, cash payments.

Bamana society is essentially divided into three broad groups, the largest of which is the *horonw* (singular *horon*), which literally means free men. This group includes farmers, soldiers, traders, and clerics. The second group, the *nyamankalaw*, includes artisans such as leather workers (*garankew*), bards (*dyeliw*), Islamic praise singers (*funew*), and blacksmiths (*numuw*).[2] While on the surface, the term *nyamankalaw* means common people, it has a much more profound meaning deriving from the words *nyama* (power, vital life force, or energy), and *kalaw* (handles). *Nyama* in *Bamanan-kan* can also mean trash or feces, but this meaning is not disconnected from the former one, since excrement contains an important part of the vital life force, *nyama*, of the animal that ejected it. Zahan best elucidates the etymology of *nyamankalaw* when he describes it as deriving from the sense of "handles of *nyama*." By extension this implies that the *nyamankalaw* are handlers of power, handlers of the life forces and energy that pervade all creation.[3]

Illus. 1.
The late master sculptor-blacksmith Siriman Fané (left), holding a recently sculpted *Tyi Wara* antelope headdress, and his nephew, Bafing Kané (right), in their forge. Village of Koké, Segou region (Cercle of Segou), 1970.

All members of the *nyamankalaw* group occupy a unique position in Bamana society not only because of their specialized skills, but more importantly because they possess the powers to control *nyama* and to use it for a variety of purposes. As a consequence, blacksmiths are viewed as powerful members of the community, and occupy a distinct position that sets them apart. Smiths are thus a caste within a caste, as McNaughton explains, and their specialized powers give them access to vast amounts of *nyama*, and contact with a pantheon of spirits. As a result, they not only sculpt wood and forge iron, but also function as healers, leaders in the *dyow* (initiation societies), and as powerful agents in dealing with sorcery. These characteristics place smiths in a position in which they are simultaneously respected and feared to varying degrees.[4]

Illus. 2.
Bamana bards (*dyeliw*) in the Segou region (Cercle of Segou), 1969.

The third social group consists of *dyonw* (slaves) and their descendants, *wolosow*. Although indigenous slavery was abolished early in the twentieth century by the French, *wolosow* are still viewed as occupying a lower social status in modern Bamana society, and often the men work as weavers and the women as spinners.

Horonw are endogamous, and do not marry with *nyamankalaw*. The latter are also endogamous, though some intermarry with *wolosow*. Although these rules governing marriage have begun to break down in urban centers such as Mali's capital, Bamako, they are still widely observed in rural villages.[5]

Illus. 3.
The late Bomama, a Bamana bard (*dyeli*) from the Segou region (Cercle of Macina), playing a stringed instrument fashioned from an oil can, 1970.

Bamana villages are called *duguw*, a word whose basic meaning is that of land. Villages in turn are comprised of compounds, often set off in the eastern Bamana country by mud brick walls. In this region, houses are usually rectangular and constructed of mud brick with roofs of wooden poles overlaid with dried mud. In the western and southern Bamana country, houses are usually round with thatch roofs. However, in recent years, rectangular mud brick construction has been increasingly adopted in this area.

Illus. 4.
The mud brick village of Boussin in the eastern Bamana country. Segou region (Cercle of Segou), 1968.

Illus. 5.
A family compound (*goua*) in the village of Tiebasa, whose doors are equipped with sculpted locks.
Fouladougou Arbala region (Cercle of Kita), 1970.

The extended family among the Bamana is called *blo-da* (vestibule doorway) because a single entrance leads to its large compound, known as a *dou* or *lou*. The latter in turn is subdivided into *gouaw* (households), which are nuclear family areas, often set off by walls. The *blo-da* is headed by a *fa* (father), who is the eldest male in the oldest generation. Each *goua* is headed by a *goua tigui* (home leader), who essentially is the male head of household. The *fa*, usually either a father or uncle to all the household heads, has ultimate authority over the extended family's economic assets. However, he is advised by his sons and nephews, and even grandsons and grand-nephews once they are circumcised and of age. The *fa* also has authority over the *foro-ba* (large field) which produces most of the extended family's annual cereal harvest, and oversees the family's livestock and all wealth that accumulates as a result of common labor. His first wife plays a major social role in that she arbitrates disputes among the women of the *blo-da* and equitably assigns communal work responsibilities to them. First wives also assist their husbands with the sale of the domestic stock products such as milk and meat. Older women of the *blo-da* frequently recount legends and fables to children that often carry important lessons about social conduct and responsibilities. [6]

Male household heads often have small fields in which they can cultivate crops for sale or barter. However, the principal assets of an extended family rest with the harvest of the *foro-ba*, over which the *fa* has significant control.

Illus. 6.
Bamana elders (*tyékorobaw*). Village of Ngoloba, Segou region (Cercle of Segou), 1969.

4

Bamana family patronyms are known as *diamouw*, and are usually associated with animal or vegetable totems known collectively as *tanaw* or *tenéw*. Several patronyms may share the same totemic animal, and a given patronym may have a differing totem depending on the region. Some patronyms and their totems are as follows: Coulibaly (hippopotamus, fish, mole-cricket, striped rat, or antelope), Cissé (python), Dembélé (black dog, panther, or red monkey), Diarra (lion, tree-*Bombax costatum*, or iguana), Doukouré (python), Dramé (python), Mariko (crocodile), Niaré (python), Ouattara (leopard), Samaké (elephant), Tounkara (tree-*Bombax costatum*), Traoré (black monkey, crocodile, or spitting cobra). Blacksmith patronyms include Coulibaly, Fané, Kané, and Kanté.[7]

Illus. 7.
Bamana men and women weeding a maize field. Mande region (Cercle of Kangaba), 1970 (Photograph by Marli Shamir).

The development of a cash economy and wage-earning opportunities under French colonial rule had major consequences for an agrarian society whose principal assets were controlled by the eldest male of a lineage. By earning wages, younger men were able to both escape the authority of the ruling gerontocracy and accumulate assets that would not have been possible had they followed a traditional Bamana way of life. Many shared these monetary assets with their fathers, who in turn acquired livestock and luxury items for their families. However, in so doing, fathers compromised their authority over their sons, whose wage earning conferred considerable social independence.

Illus. 8.
Bamana men and women harvesting and threshing. Mande region (Cercle of Kangaba), 1970 (Photograph by Marli Shamir).

The departure of so many young men for wage-earning opportunities created a manpower problem for extended families dependent on male labor for cultivating the family fields. Many rural Bamana families solved this problem by using some of the cash given to them by wage-earning sons to hire farm laborers. This in turn led to the further expansion of the cash economy into rural areas.[8]

During the eighteenth century, the Bamana developed a powerful political state around Segou on the Middle Niger. Founded by Mamari (Biton) Coulibaly, it evolved into a warrior state headed by a war chief or ruler (*fama*), and depended on a soldier class known as the *ton-dyonw* (slaves of the association). Although state power in Segou derived in part from taxes and agricultural productivity, it also drew much of its strength from the capture and sale of slaves. This latter source of wealth required both a permanent warrior class and frequent successful military campaigns through which slaves could be captured. Slaves were either incorporated into state institutions such as the army and the ruler's farms, or else sold. Slaves were generally sold to Marka (Maraka) merchants, who for the most part were Moslems. Descendants of pre-Bamana Soninké settlers of the Middle Niger, the Marka maintained extensive trade networks throughout West Africa on which the Segou kingdom greatly depended. Slaves were sent south and west to the coast, sold internally in West Africa, or shipped to trans-Saharan markets. In return for these slaves, the *fama* obtained horses, firearms, and luxury goods. However, it was the exchange of slaves for horses and firearms that was crucial to the survival of the Segou warrior state. For these assets gave Segou an enormous military advantage over its neighbors.[9]

5

Illus. 9.
Bamana woman treating shea butter nuts (*Vitellaria paradoxa*). Mande region (Cercle of Kangaba), 1970 (Photograph by Marli Shamir).

To the northwest of Segou, a second Bamana state, Kaarta, emerged in the eighteenth century. Less successful than Segou at state building, it nonetheless became a powerful force in the borderlands where the savanna is transformed into sahel. Centrifugal to both Segou and Kaarta were other Bamana regions such as the Bélédougou and the Baninko, where powerful chiefs maintained relative independence through a combination of shrewd political maneuvering, military resistance, and the payment of tribute.

Bamanaya

The Bamana rulers of Segou were in effect priest-kings because they presided over the cults of a state religion. However, this religion was not centrally administered nor adherence to orthodoxy enforced by the *fama* and his officials. Rather, the success of Segou's rulers at maintaining security over much of the Bamana country created a favorable environment in which powerful integrative social forces fostered the standardization of essential religious and philosophical beliefs and their many external manifestations. These in turn created a way of life and an understanding of the world to which the Bamana refer as *Bamanaya*. This term does not denote an ethnic group in the strictest sense. Rather it refers to a totality of beliefs and a lifestyle that can be embraced by other peoples such as the Minianka.

Illus. 10.
Bamana hunter (*donsoké*) from the Bélédougou region (Cercle of Kolokani) wearing attire that expresses some of the values of *Bamanaya*, 1967.

Confounding matters is the fact that during the twentieth century, the language *Bamanan-kan* became the lingua franca of what is now the modern political state of Mali. There are many who identify themselves as Bamana because they speak the language, but who do not, in fact, adhere to *Bamanaya*. *Bamanaya* therefore encompasses more than language, and is centered on essential beliefs and a mode of living that is accessible even to those beyond the geographic frontiers of the Bamana country.[10]

There is within *Bamanaya* itself local variations in belief patterns and ritual practices that have resulted from divergent evolutionary forces and cross-cultural contributions. Yet the essentials remain fairly uniform from one geographic area to another, as does the central feature of offering blood sacrifices to ritual objects known as *boliw* (singular *boli*). These objects are created in a variety of forms, and possess powerful *nyama*-infused encrusted surfaces consisting of a heterogeneous mixture of elements.[11]

Illus. 11.
Bamana elder (*tyékoroba*) wearing a mud cloth (*bokolanfini*) tunic. Banimounitie region (Cercle of Bougouni), 1969 (Photograph by Marli Shamir).

Bamanaya cannot be viewed as an entity completely uninfluenced by other belief patterns and ways of life. For many centuries, Moslem communities existed among the Bamana. These largely consisted of trading groups such as the Marka, who were essential to the economic well-being of the Segovian military state, and upon whom the rulers of Segou often depended for counsel and advice. Thus, the cultural exchanges between Islam and *Bamanaya* extend back many centuries, and helped shape the characteristics of both in modern Mali.

It was not until 1864 that *Bamanaya* was brought into direct open conflict with Islam. In that year, El Hadj Omar Tall, the Tukulor religious warrior, launched a jihad against the Segovian state and conquered it. Two years later, his son, Amadou Tall, became the ruler of Segou until 1890, when the French under General Louis Archinard drove him out. The Tukulor unsuccessfully tried to convert the Bamana to Islam by force. Yet, their presence in a world dominated by *Bamanaya* resulted in belief exchanges between the latter and Islam. These exchanges also occurred in the Bamana country to the south and west of Segou where the Dyula imam warrior, Samory Touré, launched military operations during the 1880s.[12]

Illus. 12.
Bamana hunter (*donsoké*) with indigenously made percussion hammer rifle and ax. Banimounitie region (Cercle of Bougouni), 1968.

Islam received its greatest impetus among the Bamana under French colonial rule. The French referred to the Bamana as the Bambara, based on information provided to them by Moslem informants. This name is derived from the *bamanan-kan* words *u banna u bara la* (they refused among themselves). The name Bamana has a similar meaning, and comes from the words *min banna a ma na* (those who refused their master).[13] In both instances, the name refers to Bamana refusal to accept Islam. Despite this refusal, Islam influenced *Bamanaya* over the centuries, and modified many of its elements. Simultaneously, *Bamanaya* influenced local Islam, and in so doing altered it considerably. These exchanges especially intensified during the period of French colonial rule, ultimately leading to the decline of *Bamanaya*, and the ascent of Islam.

The reasons for Islam's success among the Bamana during the twentieth century are several and complex. Under the French, peace and security generally prevailed over much of what is now Mali. In such an environment, and spurred on by colonial economic initiatives, a cash economy rapidly developed and merchant capitalism greatly expanded. For centuries, the latter had been controlled by elaborate networks of Moslem traders. Thus, under colonial rule, Islam became a facilitator of the expansion of merchant capitalism, and provided it with a legitimacy that had a longstanding historical basis. As increasing numbers of Bamana were drawn to the cash economy and merchant capitalism, so too were they attracted to Islam. The supra-ethnic character of Islam and the monopoly its scholars had over literacy and education gave its adherents enormous advantages when involved in long-distance trade.[14]

In addition to these factors, wage-earning possibilities rapidly expanded for the Bamana both in administrative centers and elsewhere in West Africa. Young men began leaving their villages for jobs as far away as the Ivory Coast. Even when seasonal, such employment broke the economic control of the Bamana ruling gerontocracy that heretofore had absolute authority over family and village wealth. The adoption of Islam by these young, wage-earning men served to release them from the political, judicial, and religious authority of this gerontocracy. Their physical absence from home during important periods of the year also made it increasingly difficult for villages to sustain the vitality of initiation societies and cults (*dyow*), thus leading to a weakening of *Bamanaya*.[15]

Village elders were hard put to deny wage-earning possibilities for younger men since the elders were often major material beneficiaries. Thus, the cumulative negative impact on *Bamanaya*, a system based on a local subsistence economy, derived not merely from Islam, but also from those changed economic circumstances that fostered its adoption.

Illus. 13.
The great mud brick mosque at Mopti in central Mali, 1967.

Finally, the French actively promoted Islam during the initial phase of colonial rule. Later, fearing political challenges from pan-Islamic movements, they partially reversed this policy. Islam and its various *tariqas* (brotherhoods), however, continued to draw new adherents from among the Bamana because they served as broad-based organizations through which opposition to colonial rule could be expressed. Thus, for many Bamana, Islam was a better means through which to refuse submission to a foreign colonial master than *Bamanaya*. Later, Moslem religious leaders vigorously proselytized Islam among the Bamana, while successive Malian governments gave the religion a preferred status through special considerations.[16]

Illus. 14.
Recently excised girls. Village of Boussin, Segou region (Cercle of Segou), 1969.

Tonw and Dyow

Age-grade associations, *tonw*, still play an important role in the life of rural Bamana villages. Historically, men were often circumcised at the age of twenty or so, though in recent times, boys undergo the operation between the ages of ten and twelve. Once circumcised, young men became members of a *ton*, and remained so until they married, which was usually in their early thirties. Unmarried women of the same age groups also belonged to *tonw* of their own. Circumcision and excision at younger ages, and earlier marriage have greatly altered the age configuration of *tonw*. Today, most members are either teenagers or in their twenties. *Tonw* engage in communal labor, often for charitable purposes, for the well-being of the community, or to acquire assets that can support other group activities. *Tonw* also organize public entertainments that consist of *koteba* (theatrical performances) and dances with masks and puppets, referred to in the eastern Bamana area as *sogow*. *Tonw* are complex social organizations comprised of several age sets known as *flan-bo-low* which are segregated according to gender. However, male and female *flan-bo-low* are matched, and engage in cooperative endeavors. *Ton* membership confers an important social identity on young Bamana men and women as well as access to social, emotional, and economic support in times of need.[17]

Illus. 16.
Sigikoun (buffalo head) performer during a *ton* celebration. Village of Sogonafing, Djitoumou region (Cercle of Bamako), 1970.

Illus. 15.
Recently circumcised boys. Sinzani (Sansanding), Segou region (Cercle of Segou), 1969.

The Bamana possess a number of initiation societies or associations, six of which were once widespread, and others which are confined to specific regions. These associations are collectively referred to as *dyow*. The word *dyo* (*dyon*) means "slave," an allusion to the fact that members were perceived as being liberated after periods of rigorous initiation. The six major *dyow* have been described by several scholars, although the amount of information about each varies considerably.

The *N'Tomo* and the *Korè* have been exhaustively described by Zahan, and the *Komo* by a number of authors. The *Tyi Wara* has been carefully documented by Imperato and Zahan, and the *Nama* commented on by Brett-Smith, Monteil, Tauxier, and de Zeltner.[18] The *Kono*, while mentioned by a number of scholars, has not been described in any great detail by those who observed it while it still widely functioned. In recent years, the *Nya* cult of the neighboring Minianka in which decreasing numbers of people participate has been closely studied by Colleyn.[19]

Illus. 17.
The *Zantegeba* masquerade, representing the baboon or lion.
Village of Sogonafing, Djitoumou region (Cercle of Bamako),
1970.

Illus. 18.
N'Tomo dancer. Village of Sirakoro, Djitoumou region
(Cercle of Bamako), 1969.

The six major *dyow* just mentioned generally restrict membership to men, and were widely distributed throughout the Bamana country. However, there were and still are a number of *dyow* for women, whose geographic distribution is much more limited. Over three quarters of a century ago, Henry observed the *Mousso Ka Dyiri* association for women in the southeastern Bamana country.[20] In the 1950s, Paques, who worked in the western and central regions, mentioned three such *dyow, Niagua, Kulukuto,* and *Dyide.*[21] More recently, some of the women's *dyow* have been described in greater detail as they relate to health and medical care.[22]

In addition to these *dyow*, there are others that are of local importance such as the *Dyo* and the *Gouan.* They once flourished in the southern Bamana country, and still remain functional in limited areas. Of significance is the fact that women are admitted to both of these societies.

McNaughton cogently defines the *dyow* as religious, political, judicial, and philosophical associations whose chief aim was the maintenance of social, spiritual, and economic harmony.[23] Zahan has described the *N'Tomo, Komo, Nama, Kono, Tyi Wara,* and *Korè* as links in a chain that led to the progressive

acquisition of wisdom and knowledge. Additionally, initiation exposes members to an enormous corpus of information dealing with the Bamana world view and man's role in the universal order. Thus, each association and all of them in concert serve as powerful instruments for the maintenance of social control, law, and order. The *N'Tomo* is, in a sense, the prefatory association through which the non-circumcised are initiated into the *Komo*, which acts as a village and even regional police force, punishing murderers, thieves, debtors, and sorcerers. The *Nama* is an anti-sorcery association, one of whose objectives is man's physical perfection. The *Kono* is a complementary association to the *Komo* through which all human activity is monitored by means of omnipresent powers. The *Tyi Wara*, the least secretive of the *dyow*, in the sense that women and children are permitted to witness its public rituals, is concerned with agriculture. The *Korè* is the highest level of initiation in many areas of the Bamana country, consisting of multiple hierarchical levels, passage through which brings man into union with the creator and enables him to conquer death through reincarnation. It also enables men to achieve spiritual perfection.

Illus. 19.
Young *N'Tomo* masquerader. Village of Boussin, Segou region (Cercle of Segou), 1969.

Illus. 20.
***Komo* sanctuary. Village of Djigila, Fouladougou Arbala region (Cercle of Kita), 1970.**

The *dyow* gradually fell into decline under the joint influences of conversion to Islam, colonial rule, and the exposure of younger generations to external cultural and social values and a cash economy. Tauxier, for example, details the inherent conflict between the objectives of colonial rule and the *Komo* society. This conflict had its roots in two characteristics of the *Komo*. First it was a secret society, by definition dangerous to the colonial authorities, and second it was a powerful political and judicial group that could potentially crystalize a revolt against colonial rule. Initially, the French adopted a modified tolerant attitude, going so far as to allow non-Moslem Bamana to swear by the *Komo* during judicial procedures. But eventually chiefs of the *Komo* challenged the French in political matters, and the latter did not hesitate to resort to destroying the visible elements of this *dyow* and intimidating its members. By the 1920s, the *Komo* was almost uniquely a religious association, having been divested of its political and judicial functions. [24] To combat the political threat posed by the *dyow*, the French initially supported the spread of Islam through direct financial subsidies for the construction of mosques and the establishment of koranic schools.

Although these actions of the colonial government had a strong negative impact on the *dyow*, they were not as significant as the effects of a newly created cash economy. Initiation was both costly and time-consuming. Dieterlen, for example, documented the demise of *Komo* branches because people viewed initiation as too expensive.[25] Such a perception, however, probably occurred against background in which belief in the *Komo* had dwindled. More importantly, young men in many villages were faced with choices. They could spend the long months of a dry season involved with the rites and rituals of initiation societies whose relevancy was rapidly dwindling, or they could use the time to work in the cash economy, often on the coast, and thereby improve their material well-being. Many opted for the latter. In addition, some young men espoused Islam, not so much out of fervent conviction, but as a means of escaping from the tight social, economic, and political control of the Bamana gerontocracy. [26]

Illus. 21.
Manya shrine in a Minianka village. Miniankala region
(Cercle of Koutiala), 1967.

Symbols prominent in *dyow* instruction are often found on door locks. The prominent necks on some locks symbolize the instruction given by the *Komo*. The supraclavicular spaces on either side of it, called *kolow* (wells), are important symbols of sexual and intellectual passion.[27] Bamana men are especially attracted to women, for example, who have deep and visible supraclavicular spaces.[28] The neck also represents honesty and integrity. When the Bamana say that one does not have a neck, they mean that someone does not keep promises. The *Komo* masquerader refers to his neck when speaking to young initiates by saying, "The tree around the wells (*kolow*) is stunted, but its sprouts (offspring) are numerous." This refers to the neck as a fertile source of instruction, and to the initiates as willing students of *Komo* knowledge.[29]

Illus. 22.
Bamana hunters (*donsokéw*) from the Banimounitie region
(Cercle of Bougouni) with a preserved and decorated crocodile,
a powerful anti-sorcery symbol. City of Bamako, 1969.

The jaws of the crocodile are closely associated with the anti-sorcery and anti-nefarious *nyama* powers of the *Komo*. Most *Komo* masks consist of a dome and large open crocodile jaws with sculpted teeth. This open mouth symbolizes the power of the crocodile to destroy sorcery and dangerous *nyama*, and is depicted in certain locks by two horn-like structures above the head. The *Komo* mask also represents the mythical crocodile that stowed away the ark of creation in the pond belonging to *Faro*, an important Bamana deity.[30] The anti-sorcery powers of the crocodile, and by inference of the *Komo* and *Faro*, are represented by the pointed triangular flaps of the *bamada* (crocodile mouth) hat worn by *Komo* leaders (*Komo tiguiw*) and Bamana elders.[31] These flaps simultaneously depict the wings of the swallow (*nanalékou*), *Faro's* aerial messenger.[32] These varying representations of the crocodile and the swallow are complementary, and ultimately refer to supernatural powers capable of preventing and destroying sorcery and sorcerers, and protecting people from nefarious *nyama*.

Illus. 23.
Bamana man (left) wearing a *bamada* hat representing both the crocodile's mouth and the swallow's wings (Reprinted from Abdon-Eugène Mage. *Voyage dans le Soudan Occidental.* Paris: Librairie de L. Hachette et Cie, 1868).

THE LEGENDS OF CREATION

A large corpus of metaphysical and religious beliefs once served as the foundations of traditional Bamana society. This corpus has either disappeared or else has been markedly altered in recent decades in many areas. Yet, its essential elements are often still integrated into Bamana representational art forms. Part of these beliefs consists of the story of creation, of which there are several versions. Scholars such as de Ganay, Dieterlen, Paques, and Zahan have provided detailed descriptions of the story of creation as they recorded it in various regions.[33] In 1963, Zahan published a succinct overview of the creation legends as documented by all of these researchers.[34] This story and all of the events which emanate from it represent, to a certain degree, ideal constructs. They define the world and the conduct of human affairs according to ideal norms that are rarely found in reality.

The creation legend known to the southern Bamana is strikingly depersonalized compared to its analogue in the central and northern areas.[35] While the legend around Segou, the Baninko, and even in certain areas of Bougouni contains supernatural personalities embodying known human virtues and weaknesses, the southern legend primarily revolves around nonhuman beings and forces. The southern Bamana believe in a supreme being who created man in the image of his finger. God is heat, stillness, and silence, and true creation, known as *manazo*, emanated from Him. He created all things through His vibrating spirit known as *yo*, and through His index finger. His first creation was fire that is also light, heat, sound, movement, and a generating power. This fire formed Venus (*sigi lolo*), the buffalo star, also known as the star of circumcision. Venus existed long before any other created thing, and contained all future creation. Eventually the earth appeared, containing moisture as a humid principle. The sky, symbolized by Venus, and the earth were then connected to one another by the *banagolo* tree that had seventeen branches. This tree is symbolized on earth today by the *bana* tree (*Ceiba pentandra*). It is a ladder over which the *ni* component of the human soul ascends to heaven at the time of death, while the *dya* or double of the soul resides in the family altar. The *ni* may later come down from heaven and enter the womb of a pregnant female member of the family, thus reincarnating an ancestor. Sacrifices are made to ancestors in order to nourish them, and they in turn reward their kin on earth with fertility and rain. The seventeen equal branches of the *bana* tree represent eight twin ancestor couples plus God at the top. The couple at the bottom represents the earth, and the seven others the heavens.

God and the earth are connected by a continuous line formed by this succession of men and women. A step-like line within this vertical structure symbolizes the python moving forward, expanding and transforming life. This line connecting the vertical levels of ancestors finds expression in woven cloth depicting three parallel lines of alternating black and white squares. These three lines also refer to the python that represents a continuous route of blood and fertility. The mythical python, represented by earthly ones, was created by the rays of the sun falling on the earth. It is viewed as being in perpetual movement between the humid earth and the sky. Its head symbolizes God, and is often depicted at the base of door locks.

The *bana* tree connects to seven heavens that eventually lead to God whose direction is indicated by the rainbow. The first heaven is that of scorpions and twins. Both are symbolically associated with rain and fertility. The seventh heaven is that of the white cock. His sounds, which are fertility blessings, descend through the other heavens to earth, picking up the powers of each heaven en route. The southern Bamana view the white cock as the best animal for making sacrifices to ancestors.

The first fire eventually entered a stone, but also gave a portion of itself to every living thing. While the fire in every living being eventually lessens and death ensues, that in stone does not. Thus, stone is the perpetual abode of the first fire. The stone in which the first fire resided was in the middle of a lake. Four first signs came forth from the fire, setting up the cardinal points of the earth. From these developed *Pemba* (*Bemba*), viewed by the southern Bamana as the first human ancestor. As will be seen further on, *Pemba* is regarded by other Bamana as God. All newly created things had four parts: head, neck, stomach, and legs. *Pemba*, the image of the stone which is also fire, was derived from God's fingernail. He went to the east, and from him came a second sign in the form of a trident. It was the neck, and it went to the north and is considered the earth, derived from the second finger of God. A third sign emanated from God's third finger, and went to the west. It is both the element water and the stomach or heart. From it came a double sign in the form of a bird's beak, constituting the legs and air. It was these four principal signs that then created man near the lake. Thus, he is composed of four signs: fire, earth, water, and air, and seven parts, head, stomach, vertebral column, two arms, and two legs.[36]

Illus. 24.
Antelope headdresses representing *Tyi Wara*, the Bamana deity who taught men how to farm. Village of Boussin, Segou region (Cercle of Segou), 1970.

Illus. 25.
Tyi Wara performers depicting the Bamana deity of agriculture who was the son of *Mouso Koroni Koundyé* and the cobra. Village of Djigila, Fouladougou Arbala region (Cercle of Kita), 1970.

A much more personalized creation legend is found among the northern Bamana as described by Zahan. [37] They believe in a supreme being known by a number of names such as *N'gala* and *Pemba* (*Bemba*). Closely associated with him and with the act of creation are several supernatural beings. Prominent among them are *Mouso Koroni Koundyé* or *Nyalé*, *Faro*, and *Ndomadyiri*. From a certain perspective, these beings are also diverse manifestations of God. During the first phase of creation, known as *dali folo*, the earth was devoid of living things, and God manifested himself as a grain (*kise*) known as *Pemba*. A *balanza* tree (*Acacia albida*) grew from this seed, but when it became fully grown, it withered and fell to the ground. Eventually, all that remained was a long beam of wood, known as *Pembélé*. This wooden beam secreted mildew that accumulated beneath it. *Pembélé* mixed this mildew with his own saliva to create a new being, a female, known as *Mouso Koroni Koundyé* (little old woman with a white head).

Mouso Koroni eventually had sexual intercourse with the *Pembélé*, and in the process was mutilated. As a result, she initiated human circumcision and excision. She then engaged in the creative process, engendering vegetables, animals, and human beings, the latter then being immortal. *Mouso Koroni* also had intercourse with the cobra, and gave birth to *Tyi Wara*, a half-man, half-animal deity who taught men how to farm. However, her creativity was generally characterized by disorder, confusion, and haste. This is excused by some Bamana on the grounds that she wanted to people the earth with beings as rapidly as possible. Finally, *Mouso Koroni* planted the *Pembélé* in the ground, and he became a tree once again. Men worshipped *Pemba*, now a *balanza* tree, who eventually introduced them to death. In time, men transferred their worship to *Faro*, another supernatural being and manifestation of God, who is the master of water.

Illus. 26.
Dancer mimicking the half-man, half-animal, *Tyi Wara*,
teaching men to till the soil. Village of Djigila,
Fouladougou Arbala region (Cercle of Kita), 1970.

As Zahan points out, some Bamana believe that *Mouso Koroni* either disappeared or died at this point, after spending a wretched life on earth authoring disorder. Others, however, believe that she continues to live, the personification of air, wind, and fire. She is also the "mother of magic," the first sorcerer, and as such is called by another name, *Nyalé*.

Mouso Koroni was originally created with a soul that had two parts, like those of all human beings, the *ni*, and its shadow, the *dya*. But at the time of her creation, while God gave her the *ni*, he entrusted its double, the *dya*, to *Faro*. Thus, *Mouso Koroni* was incomplete from the moment of her creation.

Nonetheless, she authored the first phase of creation, characterized by prodigious growth and fertility. As Zahan notes, as *Nyalé*, she gives strength to newborns and hastens the ripening of grain. She is the source of all human ideas, which have been or will be given to man, and represents energy, activity, and desire. But she is also the source of all malice, misunderstanding, treachery, and sorcery. She is an extravagant being, unruly, uncontrolled, and excessive. She causes everything to proliferate, but in an uncontrolled manner. Yet, her creative energies extend into every facet of the earth and cosmos. She invented hair styling, jewelry, and instructed humans to use facial scarifications to distinguish men from women in the era before speech was invented.[38] The trajectory of her worldly travels, represented on the surfaces of locks as chevrons, also symbolizes the path of Venus (*sigi lolo*), the morning star. As explained by de Ganay, Bamana recognition of the relationship between her travels, the path of Venus, and her initiation of circumcision and excision accounts for the performance of these operations when the star is at its brightest.[39]

In traveling throughout the world, *Mouso Koroni* was pursued by her husband, *Pemba*. During his pursuit of her, he created air, fire, water and earth, and sickness and death. According to de Ganay, she traveled west-south-east-north, while *Faro*, who was enlisted by *Pemba* to control her, traveled east, west, south, and north.[40] His journeys are also depicted on the surfaces of locks by chevrons.

In entrusting *Mouso Koroni's dya* to *Faro*, God in effect set limits on the amount of chaos in the world. He also deprived the primordial female being of coherence, and made her defective. It could be cogently argued that the ancient Bamana conceived of this component of the legend to rationalize woman's imposed inferior position in their society and the necessity for male dominance. Some Bamana believe that *Mouso Koroni* died after the first phase of creation. According to a popular legend, she was reduced to starvation and misery. One day an old woman, out of pity, gave her a millet cake to eat. As she raised it to her mouth, a large black scorpion (*dyonkomi*) emerged and stung her. Falling backward as she died, she crushed the scorpion, which was later discovered by the blacksmiths who were called to examine her. They attached a cord to the tail of the scorpion, tied it to her leg, and then buried both together.

Illus. 27.
Nama Koroni Koun
(little old hyena head)
masquerader who
often accompanies
the *Tyi Wara*
performers.
Village of Djigila,
Fouladougou Arbala
region (Cercle of Kita),
1970.

Illus. 28.
Sogo koun
(antelope head)
masquerade.
Village of
Boussin, Segou
region (Cercle of
Segou), 1969.

16

The second phase of creation, called *dali flani*, was dominated by *Faro* (water hole) and *Ndomadyiri* (wood divinity). The former represents equilibrium, and the latter stability. *Faro* is viewed by the Bamana as the most powerful of the supernatural beings. His physical characteristics include a white feminine face, long, smooth black hair, black eyes, no external ears, a body surface equally covered by skin and copper, and a webbed tail.[41] *Faro* is androgynous, and, according to legend, gave birth to twins.[42] In some legends, he stole his white face from a lesser divinity, *Téliko*, an albino, who is today symbolized by whirlwinds.[43] *Faro* lives in water, and is associated with thunder, lightening, rain, and rainbows. His role is to perfect the world, organize it, put it in equilibrium, and give it eternal life. *Faro* was born of God's vaporous breath, from a bubble of his saliva while God was pronouncing the words of creation. *Faro* is also the visible countenance of God, a countenance that is white. *Faro* is, in a sense, God's word, but during this second phase of creation, this word was unintelligible to humans, consisting of a language in which all words were connected. This language of continuous sound began when *Pemba*, angered by *Mouso Koroni's* behavior, cut her on the neck. She let out a continuous sound in response to the pain that became the only language during the first phase of creation.[44]

It was *Ndomadyiri*, the divine blacksmith, the third supernatural person after *Mouso Koroni* and *Faro*, who made this primordial word into useful language. He is what is left, the earth, after the evaporation of water (*Faro*) due to the action of the wind (*Nyalé*). This provokes the notion of fixity, of remaining in place after the withdrawal of his previous associations. So

the Bamana see him symbolized in trees, fixed and powerful living beings, the source of the first life, *Mouso Koroni*. As a tree, *Ndomadyiri* is the master of herbs and remedies, and a healer, characteristics of all blacksmiths. Thus, *Ndomadyiri* is the eponymous ancestor of all blacksmiths, and the author of all healing.[45] *Faro* and *Ndomadyiri* complement one another because *Faro* represents water and rain, needed for life, while *Ndomadyiri* is the earth and fire, and possesses stability and provides man with a home.

Faro manifests himself under many forms, including crocodiles, water iguanas, goats, gazelles, and beautiful women who enter villages for the purpose of seducing young boys. He is on the crest of a swollen stream after a heavy rain, within the swirling waters of a river, and in the vapor that rises above ponds early in the morning. He is present wherever there is water, but especially inhabits deep depressions in the Niger River called *faro tyin*.[46]

The swallow (*nanalékou*) is *Faro's* aerial messenger. According to Bamana legends, this bird never steps on impure ground. Its wings are represented in the *bamada* hat worn by male elders, and are a powerful anti-sorcery symbol.[47] The *bamada* hat, also worn by the leaders of the *Komo* initiation society, consists of a central white cotton dome and two upturned triangular-shaped flaps. Besides representing the wings of the swallow, these flaps also symbolize the jaws of the crocodile, which are a powerful force against sorcery and malevolent *nyama*. The crocodile is intimately linked to *Faro* as the principal protector of his waters. It assists *Faro* in his work, and prevents his waters from being misused by undesirable humans.[48]

Faro is also associated with certain plants, especially the indigenous tomato, *ngoyo* (*Lycopersicum cerasiforme*). Its grains are arranged in multiples of seven, a number denoting twins. The Bamana believe that this fruit, when eaten by women, facilitates pregnancy through *Faro's* power, and promotes the birth of twins.[49]

The third phase of creation is that of the present, and is the stage when human beings and their desires confront one another. The formation of human societies results in confusion and disorder due to men asserting themselves and expressing their wills and emotions. *Ndomadyiri*, however, as a blacksmith, is omnipresent, stabilizing society through his supervision of its religious rites.

According to some versions of the creation legend, *Mouso Koroni*, who died after the first phase of creation, appeared again during the third phase as *Nyalé*. While the second phase was characterized by order, balance and harmony, the third phase has great potential for the disorder and confusion characteristic of the first phase because of her presence. Again, a male-dominated society, which relegates women to an inferior political and social position, produces powerful religious and metaphysical reasons for doing so.

Known in this last ongoing phase as *Nyalé*, *Mouso Koroni* represents activity, energy, mystery, desire, secrecy, and a desire for all that man wants to achieve. She is not only unbounded enthusiasm and extravagance, but also a source of fertility and creation. If left to the influences of *Nyalé* alone, man would indulge in all manner of excesses, and society would break down. That is why *Ndomadyiri* is present, to control and set limits, and *Faro* to provide equilibrium.

As Zahan explains, the Bamana legend of creation is one dominated by competing supernatural beings. *Nyalé* cannot totally disappear because as the source of creation, animation, rivalry, and very importantly, courage, the world cannot progress without her. But left alone, her influence would result in a complete breakdown of creation. Therefore, *Ndomadyiri* is needed as a counterweight of stability. In a sense, *Nyalé* and *Ndomadyiri* are diametrically opposed principles, with *Faro* providing the equilibrium necessary to balance their powers.[50]

The Bamana legends of creation contain numerous elements that are expressed in sculptural form. These are especially prominent in the overall architectonics and surface designs of door locks. Symbols of the legends about *Mouso Koroni* are common, in part because locks are largely considered to be both feminine and the property of women. These representations of *Mouso Koroni* not only recall her creativity, but also the chaos and disorder that accompanied it.

Illus. 29.
Close-up of the head of a Bamana door lock representing *Mouso Koroni Koundyé*. Bougouni region (Cercle of Bougouni). See also Figure 16 in the Catalogue section (Photograph by Marli Shamir).

They remind women that male dominance is required in order to provide society with stability and security. The architectonics of locks also incorporate legends about *Faro* and *Pemba* (*Pembélé*), but do not commonly or explicitly refer to *Ndomadyiri*, who is otherwise represented in iron sculpture and large statues, especially by the southern Bamana.[51] It is the fixation of the locks by iron nails to doors that recalls *Ndomadyiri's* role in the legend of creation, and also pyroengraved graphic signs in general of which he is the original author.[52]

Mouso Koroni is also depicted in a masquerade performed among the Bamana and Marka of the Segou region. This masquerade is presented by youth associations, and is called *dyoboli* (*dyabali*), which literally means "against the cult."[53] Masks of various styles are used during this masquerade to depict a beautiful woman who, despite her many fine physical attributes, has serious character defects. While the masquerader performs with the mask, the crowd sings variants of the following song: [54]

Oh dyoboli
How beautiful you are
dyoboli
your dress is so elegant
Oh dyoboli
How beautiful you are
dyoboli
you have come too late
The worthwhile time has passed.

Illus. 30.
Dyoboli **mask representing** *Mouso Koroni Koundyé,* **sculpted in the 1960s by the late master sculptor-blacksmith, Siriman Fané. Village of Koké, Segou region (Cercle of Segou), 1969.**

Contemporary Bamana and Marka interpret the *dyoboli koun,* as the masks are called, as meaning "the head that is hurrying to be dependable." *Dyoboli* is a beautiful woman, as evidenced by her face, coiffure, and dress, but she is also late, and therefore undependable. Beneath this superficial message is a deeper one delivered in the interests of a male-dominated society. *Dyoboli,* aware of her unusual beauty, has spurned many suitors, holding out for the best possible marriage partner. In doing so, she has disobeyed her parents and challenged the well-established custom of arranged marriages. This leaves her at risk of becoming a spinster, a tragic fate among the Bamana. Yet, there is something more than marriage being addressed here. Women are reminded that submission to male societal authority is a virtue, and that despite great beauty, they will suffer serious consequences if they choose to ignore it.[55]

These contemporary popular interpretations of the *dyoboli* masquerade make no reference to *Mouso Koroni.* This is largely accounted for by the performance of this masquerade by Moslem Marka and Bamana who have converted to Islam. Yet, at its essence, this masquerade represents *Mouso Koroni,* her rebellious and disordered behavior, and the attempts of *Pemba, Ndomadyiri,* and *Faro* to counter the consequences of her anti-social activities.[56]

Faro is sometimes depicted in sculpture, either as a small female figure with long hair, or as a figure with both human and reptilian physical features. These small statues are sometimes covered with kaolin (white clay), which, over time, and in the absence of re-application, wears off, leaving only traces of residue.[57]

SORCERY, MAGIC, AND VILLAGE PROTECTOR SPIRITS

Bamana life is suffused with a pervasive fear of *soubaw* or *soubagaw* (sorcerers) and sorcery (*soubaya*).[58] People also live in fear of the nefarious effects of *nyama*, the power, vital life force, or energy that resides in all creation. The killing of an animal, for example, releases its *nyama*, which can harm a hunter unless he performs the appropriate rituals to appease it. Sorcerers are believed to be capable of inflicting a range of illnesses and misfortunes, either on an individual or on an entire family and community. Sorcerers are especially active at night, and have a number of familiars. It is popularly believed in parts of the Bélédougou region that sorcerers are capable of transforming themselves into owls. These owls can become invisible and enter houses as a fine breath, and then drink the blood of young girls.[59] Another popular belief is that the small gray gecko (*sirantoula*) can cause leprosy. Those practicing sorcery cause the disease by placing parts of a gecko in someone's bedding or food.[60]

The Bamana are especially fearful of *kortéw*, which are small grains of cereal, bone, stone, or wood that are dispatched through the air by someone practicing sorcery. The malevolent power of these objects comes largely from the *nyama* inherent in the ritual pronouncements made over them by sorcerers. The *nyama* enters the object and infuses it with the ability to cause sickness and misfortune. Thus, as sorcery objects, *kortéw* are really substrates for the nefarious *nyama* infused in them by sorcerers. The small grains (*kenkew*) that remain after a sorcerer creates *kortéw* are also endowed with *nyama*, and can fall upon victims with the rain. The Bamana believe that both *kenkew* and *kortéw* can penetrate a victim's skin, or else enter their food or drink.[61]

The Bamana also fear actual poisons derived from either plants or animals. These are called *donkonow*, and are usually put surreptitiously into food or water. Yet, the power of these poisons is believed to originate not just from their innate properties, but more importantly from the *nyama* infused in them by a sorcerer's verbal pronouncements.[62]

Sirikounw are magical fetishes composed of animal horns, hair, hide, and cotton threads. Often carried in leather bags or suspended from a belt, they are believed to cause illness and misfortune when those practicing sorcery pronounce magical formulas over them and direct their *nyama* toward victims. *Sirikounw* can also be used for divination.

The Bamana employ a variety of strategies to prevent sorcery and to regulate *nyama*. Door locks play an important role in this broad effort, and as such, can be viewed as power objects that help prevent sorcery and regulate *nyama*. It is these functions that far outweigh their role as devices to keep out potential thieves and intruders.

Illus. 31.
Boli (right) in the form of a cow, and a *Kono* mask (left) in the early twentieth century (Reproduced from Henry, Joseph. *L'Ame d'un peuple africain*. Munster: Aschendorffschen Buchhandlung, 1910).

Boliw are magical objects that the Bambara use to assess accusations, divine guilt, and punish wrongdoers, especially sorcerers. They are created in a variety of forms including round balls, sticks and branches, human-like figures, and cows. The encrusted surfaces on them consist of a heterogeneous mixture of elements that include millet porridge, alcoholic liquids, chewed kola nuts, saliva, the blood of sacrificial animals such as chickens, goats, sheep, and cattle, and animal and human excrement. All of these encrusted surfaces are viewed by the Bamana as possessing enormous amounts of *nyama*, and thus being extremely powerful. As power objects, *boliw* are used as agents of social control, to promote the general social welfare, and to judge and punish sorcerers.[63]

Illus. 32.
***Boli* in the form of a human in the early twentieth century (Reprinted from Henry, Joseph. *L'Ame d'un peuple africain.* Munster: Aschendorffschen Buchhandlung, 1910).**

Abbé Joseph Henry, an early twentieth-century missionary of the White Fathers among the Bamana, said of *boliw* that: "Ils rendent de fait la justice." [64] In effect, they administer justice, but under the control of the old men who are their guardians. Thus, sorcery accusations and disputes, and problems brought before village elders are adjudicated through consultation with the *boliw* that belong to *dyow* such as the *Komo*. This, in effect, provides these men with a comfortable margin of protection from the consequences of their decisions. For as far as society is concerned, the *boliw* are the final, infallible, and independent arbiters of justice, capable of administering punishment and even imposing a death sentence, if necessary, by means not always fully understood. Therefore, *boliw* give society assurances that sorcerers and wayward *nyama* can be identified and neutralized in an expeditious manner.

Completing the circle of protection against sorcerers and nefarious *nyama* are *dassiriw* (village protector spirits), which reside in material supports such as trees, animals, or unusual rock formations. These spirits, which represent *Faro*, provide protection from sorcery, and counteract the *nyama* of animals, men, and inanimate objects that seek to harm a village as a whole. *Dassiriw* are also invoked in order to assist people in achieving certain objectives. Women, for example, who have difficulty becoming pregnant often petition *dassiriw* through sacrifices of millet porridge or other materials. In many villages, the *dassiri* is a baobab or acacia tree surrounded by a brush enclosure. Even if the *dassiri* resides in a tree, it can also assume the form of a crocodile (*bama*), water iguana (*kana*), land iguana (*koro*), goat (*ba*), and so on. Thus, locks depicting crocodiles, iguanas, or other animals can become material supports for *dassiriw* spirits. Regular animal and millet porridge sacrifices are made to a *dassiri*, and a ritual sacrifice is held once a year in which the entire village participates in order to renew the spirit's power.[65]

Illus. 33.
A *dassiri* village protector spirit consisting of an ancient baobab tree (*Adansonia digitata*) surrounded by a brush enclosure. Segou region (Cercle of San), 1968.

Among the Bamana, there are several types of practitioners who deal with sorcery and nefarious *nyama* and their adverse consequences. These include *furatiguiw* (herbalists), *nya bouinw* (diviners and spirit mediums), *basitiguiw* (diviners), *somaw* (spirit mediums), and *moribaw* (Koranic scholars). Some of these provide amulets and talismans to respectively protect against sorcerers and *nyama*, and to bring good fortune. The herbs used by herbalists are believed to contain innate substances capable of treating disease. However, the Bamana also believe that the ritual pronouncements made over herbs infuse them with additional powerful *nyama*, without which they would be less efficacious.[66]

GRAPHIC SIGNS

The Bamana use a number of graphic signs known as *tiw* (singular *ti*) to depict inanimate objects, natural phenomena, living beings, and abstract ideas (Illustration 35). [67] As observed by Zahan during his preliminary study of the late 1940s, these pictographs often have commonly understood meanings. However, they can also have secondary meanings understood primarily by a small number of ritual leaders. The fact that signs can express more than one meaning is explained by Zahan on the basis of their nonphonetic character and because the concepts depicted by them are parts of larger ideas. He also notes that a sign may convey differing direct meanings by region because of local religious and mythological belief variation. In addition, he relates that given individuals in the same region may interpret a sign differently based on personal psychological variations.[68] Further complicating matters is the fact that what is a direct or principal meaning in one region may be a secondary one in another.

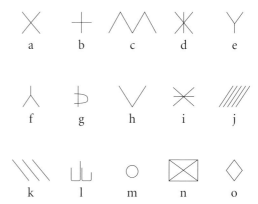

Illus. 35.
Bamana graphic signs (pictographs). (a) fertility, the universe, man, the four cardinal angles, *Pemba's* cosmic travels; (b) the four directions of cosmic space, the four cardinal points; (c) cosmic travels of *Pemba, Mouso Koroni Koundyé,* and *Faro*; the celestial path of Venus, the annual trajectory of the sun; (d) the universe; (e) the male principle; (f) the female principle; (g) the *dya* (spiritual double of a human being); (h) speech, hearing; (i) sickness or death; (j) *Pemba's* divinity; (k) all that *Pemba* entrusted to Faro, the relationship between *Pemba* and *Faro*; (l) pregnancy; (m) rain, water, *Mouso Koroni Koundyé's* tears; (n) species multiplication, fertility, four cardinal sides, limits of the universe; (o) four directions of celestial space, procreative fluids, cosmic waters, procreation (based on sources cited in the text and information provided to the author by informants in the field).

Illus. 34.
A Bamana herbalist (*furatigui*) selling herbs in one of Bamako's markets, 1968.

Although door locks have important educative, commemorative, and utilitarian purposes in Bamana society, they also serve as part of an impressive array of measures intended to confront sorcery and manage *nyama*. Unlike most other means used by the Bamana to deal with these forces, locks are highly visible and permanently displayed in public. As such, they are power objects that serve notice to both sorcerers and other malevolent supernatural forces that those who reside behind the doors also have access to more secret and powerful means of dealing with them.

On the basis of these observations, it would seem that Bamana graphic signs cannot serve as a system of mutually understood communication. However, one must be aware that the various meanings of a given sign are usually intimately connected to one another. For example, a large pyroengraved X on a door lock often represents fertility. However, it can also symbolize the universe and man, the four cardinal angles, and *Pemba's* cosmic travels when he engaged in the creative process (Illustration 35, a). The principal meaning of fertility understood in most Bamana regions is closely related to the others because it was through his cosmic travels that *Pemba* created air, fire, water, and earth. As de Ganay states, these are the basis of all fertility, both human and otherwise.[69] When the X is framed on all four sides, it still represents fertility, but more specifically species multiplication (Illustration 35, n). The lines surrounding the X refer to the limits of the universe and its four cardinal sides, known in *Bamanan-kan* as *jen seleke nani*.[70] However, more is implied here than the limits of the universe. Limits must also be set for procreation and increase in order to avoid the disorder and disharmony caused by *Mouso Koroni's* initial creative efforts. Those limits are imposed by Faro, who originally subdued *Mouso Koroni*, and who continues to provide all creation with equilibrium. Therefore, this graphic sign, while conveying the meanings of fertility and the limits of the universe, also refers to the complimentary and antagonistic characteristics of *Mouso Koroni* and *Faro*.

Similarly, chevrons (Illustration 35, c) are frequently interpreted as representing the cosmic travels of *Mouso Koroni* as she engaged in the creative process and instituted circumcision and excision. These chevrons can equally depict *Pemba's* pursuit of her, and *Faro's* cosmic travels as he organized and put equilibrium into *Mouso Koroni's* creations. Yet, this symbol can also represent the path of Venus, a planet which, when at its brightest, announces the period for circumcision and excision. Chevrons can further represent the annual trajectory of the sun, which is intimately linked to the agricultural cycle and to *Mouso Koroni's* creative efforts and those of *Faro*.[71] Therefore, while there are several meanings communicated by these chevrons, they are all closely related to one another and speak of the story of creation.[72]

Whether chevrons represent the travels of either *Pemba*, *Mouso Koroni*, or *Faro* is sometimes determined by the Bamana on the basis of the larger context in which they appear. In the lock depicted in Figure 19 in the Catalogue section, the chevrons are associated with diagonal striations, another important symbol of *Pemba*. The presence of these signs along with other sculptural symbolism makes this lock as a whole a powerful reference to the relationship between *Mouso Koroni* and *Pemba*. In other instances, however, the absence of a broader context can lead to variable interpretations of a given sign.

The interconnectedness of multiple meanings associated with single graphic signs is again demonstrated by the lozenge (Illustration 35, o). This sign represents the four directions of celestial space as opposed to the cross, which depicts those of cosmic space.[73] However, the lozenge also represents procreative fluids (semen and amniotic fluid), creative waters, and cosmic waters, ideas that are all subsets of the overarching concept of procreation as it is understood by the Bamana. Similarly, the circle (Illustration 35, m) depicts rain, water, or the tears of *Mouso Koroni* after she had been reduced to wretchedness.[74] Rain and water are both connected to agricultural fertility, as is *Mouso Koroni* through her giving birth to *Tyi Wara*, who taught men the techniques of farming. It is the central idea of agricultural fertility that holds these various meanings together and places them in close relationship to one another.

There are a large number of graphic signs known to the Bamana. Those shown in Illustration 35 represent a group frequently pyroengraved on door locks and on a variety of utilitarian objects such as wooden bowls and calabashes. The very public display of these signs underscores a Bamana intent to use them to teach and remind people about the essential religious and philosophical beliefs and values of *Bamanaya*. These graphic signs are often integrated with door lock architectonics that themselves convey powerful messages about history, legends, and required social behavior. Thus, locks serve as integrative objects that bring together graphic signs and sculpture in order to display some of the underlying beliefs and values of *Bamanaya*.

Some graphic signs, such as those employed by the *Komo* society, are not publicly displayed. Dieterlen and Cissé documented 266 *Komo* signs, which are primarily reserved for educating initiates. These signs constitute *doni dyu*, the foundation of all knowledge.[75] They represent God's thoughts, and retrace the creation of both the visible and invisible universe. With only a few exceptions, these *Komo* signs do not appear on door locks. They are usually curvilinear in character compared to the publicly displayed signs on locks that most often consist of linear and angular configurations.

The lines used in most graphic signs displayed on locks may be either single or multiple. Meaning does not vary according to this characteristic. For example, a single-lined X has the same meaning as double- and triple-lined ones. [76] Occasionally, signs may be only partially engraved on a lock's surface or else coalesced to create yet another configuration. These latter characteristics are demonstrated in Figures 27 and 49 in the Catalogue section.

The Bamana use geometricized designs on *bokolanfini* (mud cloth). Some of these partially resemble the graphic signs used on the surfaces of locks. However, their meanings are quite different.[77]

REFERENCES

1.	For an overview of the Bamana, see Labouret, Henri. *Les Manding et leur langue.* Paris: Librairie Larose, 1934; Paques, Viviana. *Les Bambara.* Paris: Presses Universitaires de France, 1954; and Tauxier, Louis. *Histoire des Bambara.* Paris: Librairie Orientaliste Paul Geuthner, 1942. Much of what is said in this text about the Bamana can be applied to other Mande peoples such as the Malinké.

2 .	The plural of Bamana nouns is generally rendered by the addition of w as a suffix. When the noun is modified, the w is added only to the modifier. An excellent detailed discussion of Bamana blacksmiths and their role in society is provided by McNaughton, Patrick R. *The Mande Blacksmiths. Knowledge, Power, and Art in West Africa.* Bloomington and Indianapolis: Indiana University Press, 1988. A recent and thorough discussion of some *nyamankalaw* is provided by Frank, Barbara E. *Mande Potters and Leather-Workers. Art and Heritage in West Africa.* Washington, DC and London: Smithsonian Institution Press, 1998.

3 .	Zahan, Dominique. *La Dialectique du verbe chez les Bambara.* Paris: Mouton & Co., 1963, 146–147.

4 .	McNaughton. *The Mande*, 19, 159.

5.	Details on the social organization of the Bamana are provided by N'Diayé, Bokar. *Groupes ethniques au Mali.* Bamako: Editions Populaires, 1970, 88–143.

6 .	Ibid., 102–104. The term *dou*, which can also mean "to eat," not only designates the extended family, but also implies that they eat from a common food source. See Zahan. *La Dialectique*, 71, note 4. The term *goua-bougou* means kitchen, and thus *goua* defines a family that uses the same kitchen. *Goua* also refers to the elevated wooden platforms on which men gather to hold discussions.

7 .	Details about Bamana totemic beliefs were recorded early in the twentieth century by Reverend Joseph Brun, a White Fathers missionary. See Brun, Joseph. Le totémisme chez quelques peuples du Soudan Occidental. *Anthropos* 1910, 5:843–869. See also Tauxier, Louis. *La Religion Bambara.* Paris: Librairie Orientaliste Paul Geuthner, 1927, 115–138.

8.	Personal observations made in the field in Mali during the 1960s and 1970s. The pattern of circular labor migration to and from West African towns and coastal economies is not unique to the rural Bamana. This pattern has been widespread among diverse rural populations of the West African savanna and sahel for many decades. For some recent studies of circular labor migration outside of Mali, see Rain, David. *Eaters of the Dry Season. Circular Labor Migration in the West African Sahel.* Boulder, CO: Westview Press, 1999; and Cordell, Dennis D., Gregory, Joel W., and Piché, Victor. *Hoe and Wage. A Social History of a Circular Migration System* in West Africa. Boulder, CO: Westview Press, 1998.

9.	The pre-colonial and colonial history of the Bamana are discussed in great detail by several authors. See Djata, Sundiata A. *The Bamana Empire by the Niger. Kingdom, Jihad and Colonization 1712–1920.* Princeton, NJ: Markus Wiener Publishers, 1997; Monteil, Charles. *Les Bambara de Ségou et du Kaarta. Etude historique, ethnographique et littéraire d'une peuplade du Soudan Français.* Paris: G.P. Maisonneuve & Larose, 1924; Roberts, Richard. *Warriors, Merchants, and Slaves. The State and the Economy in the Middle Niger Valley, 1700–1914.* Stanford, CA: Stanford University Press, 1987; and Webb, James L.A., Jr. *Desert Frontier. Ecological and Economic Change along the Western Sahel, 1600–1850.* Madison: University of Wisconsin Press, 1994.

10.	Colleyn, Jean-Paul and DeClippel, Catherine. *Bamanaya. Un'arte di vivre in Mali / Un art de vivre au Mali.* Milan: Centro Studi Archeologia Africana, 1998.

11.	See McNaughton, Patrick R. *Secret Sculptures of Komo. Art and Power in Bamana (Bambara) Initiation Societies.* Philadelphia: Institute for the Study of Human Issues, 1979; and Brett–Smith, Sarah. The Poisonous Child. *RES: Anthropology and Aesthetics* 1983, 6:47–64.

12.	Imperato, Pascal James. *Mali. A Search for Direction.* Boulder, CO : Westview Press, 1989, 30–35.

13.	Harmon, Stephen Albert. *The Expansion of Islam among the Bambara under French Rule: 1890–1940.* Ph.D. dissertation. Ann Arbor, MI: University Microfilms International, 1993, 186–187.

14.   Ibid., 44–47.

15.   Dieterlen recorded in the mid–twentieth century that some villages had difficulty sustaining initiation societies because of financial costs, and that this in turn promoted conversions to Islam. See Dieterlen, Germaine. *Essai sur la religion Bambara.* Paris: Presses Universitaires de France, 1951, 154.

16.   It has often been assumed that the change from *Bamanaya* to Islam is a gradual one characterized by long periods of syncretism. However, Yaya Diallo, a Minianka traditionalist, has documented a very rapid process sustained by Moslem proselytizers through intimidation, fear, and threats. For details on this and on the deleterious impact of these proselytizers on traditional religious beliefs and institutions, see Diallo, Yaya and Hall, Mitchell. *The Healing Drum. African Wisdom Teachings.* Rochester, Vermont: Destiny Books, 1989, 190–192.

17.   Arnoldi, Mary Jo. *Playing with Time. Art and Performance in Central Mali.* Bloomington and Indianapolis: Indiana University Press, 1995; and Imperato, Pascal James. The Dance of the Tyi Wara. *African Arts* 1970, IV(1):8–13, 71–80.

18.   Zahan, Dominique. *Sociétés d'initiation Bambara. Le N'Domo. Le Korè.* Paris: Mouton & Co., 1960; Dieterlen, Germaine and Cissé, Youssouf. *Les Fondements de la société d'initiation du Komo.* Paris: Mouton & Co., 1970; Henry, Joseph. *L'Ame d'un peuple africain. Les Bambara; leur vie psychique, éthique, sociale, religieuse.* Munster: Aschendorffschen Buchhandlung, 1910 (republished as *L'Ame d'un peuple africain. Les Bambara.* Paris: Picard, 1920); Monteil. *Les Bambara*; Tauxier, Louis. *La Religion*; Travélé, Moussa. Le Komo ou Koma. *Outre–Mer* 1929; 1:127–150, Imperato. The Dance; de Zeltner, R.P. Le culte du Nama au Soudan. *Bulletin et Memoires de la Société d'Anthropologie de Paris* 1910, 1:361–362; and Brett–Smith, Sarah C. *The Making of Bamana Sculpture. Creativity and Gender.* Cambridge: Cambridge University Press, 1994, 25, 155, 213, 262. Although the *dyow* are described here in the present tense, they are now extinct in many areas.

19.   Colleyn, Jean-Paul. *Les Chemins de Nya. Culte de possession au Mali.* Paris: Editions de l'Ecole des Hautes Etudes en Sciences Sociales, 1988.

20.   Henry. *L'Ame*, 95–96, 114.

21.   Paques. *Les Bambara*, 86.

22.   Imperato, Pascal James. The Role of Women in Traditional Healing among the Bambara of Mali. *Transactions of the Royal Society of Tropical Medicine and Hygiene* 1981, 75(6):766–770.

23.   McNaughton. *Secret Sculptures*, 3.

24.   Tauxier. *La Religion*, 281, 301.

25.   Dieterlen. *Essai*, 154.

26.   Paques, Viviana. Les Samaké. *Bulletin de l'IFAN* 1956, B, 18:369–390.

27.   Zahan. *La Dialectique*, 24.

28.   Personal observations made in the field in Mali during the 1960s and 1970s.

29.   Zahan. *La Dialectique*, 24.

30.   Dieterlen. *La Religion*, 48, and Dieterlen and Cissé. *Les Fondements*, 48.

31.   Details concerning the symbolism of these hats within the context of the *Dyo* society are given by Paques, Viviana. Bouffons sacrés du cercle de Bougouni (Soudan Français). *Journal de la Société des Africanistes* 1954, 24:63–110. See especially page 98 for a discussion of *bamada* hat symbolism.

32.   Dieterlen. *La Religion*, 48.

33.   de Ganay, Solange. II. Graphies de voyages mythiques chez les Bambara. *Africa* 1951, 21:20–23; Dieterlen. *Essai*, 1–33; Paques. Bouffons, 66–78; and Zahan, Dominique. *The Bambara.* Leiden: E.J. Brill, 1974, 1–8. During my early studies of the Bamana, I found that much of the legend of creation was still an integral part of the corpus of religious and philosophical beliefs of many. I was not then as familiar with the studies of de Ganay, Dieterlen, Paques, and Zahan as I later became. On subsequent careful study of their works, I discovered that they had both accurately and insightfully documented these beliefs. Elders in three villages of the Cercle of Segou, Konodimini, Péléngana, and Banankoroni recalled Dieterlen's work among them almost two decades earlier, and her profound level of knowledge of their beliefs and way of life.

34.   Zahan. *La Dialectique*, 116–120.

35.   Paques. Bouffons, 66–78.

24

36.   Ibid.

37.   Zahan. *The Bambara*, 1–8.

38.   For details on *Mouso Koroni's* creative activities, see Dieterlen. *Essai*, 16–19.

39.   de Ganay II. Graphies, 22

40.   Ibid., 21–22.

41.   Dieterlen. *Essai*, 41–42.

42.   Ibid., 42.

43.   *Teliko*, the albino divinity of the air, originally challenged *Faro's* power and authority, but was defeated by the latter. See Dieterlen. *Essai*, 25–26; and Paques. *Les Bambara*, 83. One afternoon in 1970, I was seated under a tree with the elders of the village of Zambougou in the Arrondissement of Markala. As we spoke, a small whirlwind passed by. One of them looked at me, smiled, and said, "*Teliko*." He then discussed this lesser divinity, told me of his foolish challenge to *Faro*, and the loss of his white face.

44.   Zahan. *La Dialectique*, 16.

45.   Zahan. *The Bambara*, 4.

46.   Dieterlen. *Essai*, 44–47. Over time, the Bamana have assimilated the form of the crocodile into that of the iguana in representational sculpture. Thus, iguanas are frequently viewed as equally powerful avatars for *Faro* as crocodiles. See Paques. Bouffons, 77. Iguanas and other lizards can also symbolize fertility and good fortune. See Brett-Smith. *The Making*, 296.

47.   Dieterlen. *Essai*, 48.

48.   Ibid.

49.   Ibid.

50.   Zahan. *The Bambara*, 5.

51.   For wooden and iron sculptural representations of *Mouso Koroni* and *Ndomadyiri* among the southern Bamana, see Imperato, Pascal James. *Buffoons, Queens and Wooden Horsemen. The Dyo and Gouan Societies of the Bambara of Mali.* New York: Kilima House Publishers, 1983.

52.   *Ndomadyiri* is the master of writing and teaching. He is the *kala* (to teach) *tigui* (chief). In his blacksmith role, he was the first to create the graphic signs used by the Bamana. See Zahan. *La Dialectique*, 120.

53.   Tesi, Paule. *Introduction à l'étude des serrures Bambara.* Memoire de maîtrise. Paris, 1972, 42 (microfiche).

54.   For details on the contemporary *dyoboli* (*dyabali*) masquerade, see Imperato, Pascal James. The Depiction of Beautiful Women in Malian Youth Association Masquerades. *African Arts* 1994, XXVII(1):58–65, 95.

55.   Ibid.

56.   Interviews with Siriman Fané and Bafing Kané, master sculptor–blacksmiths, Koké, Arrondissement of Markala, Cercle of Segou, Mali, 1970–1974. Bafing Kané died in 1996, while his uncle, Siriman Fané, died several years before.

57.   Interviews with Moussa Coulibaly, master sculptor–blacksmith, Touganabougou, Arrondissement of Markala, Cercle of Segou, Mali, 1968–1974. Moussa Coulibaly died in the early 1990s.

58.   The term s*oubaga* derives from the *Bamanan–kan* words *sou* (night) and *baga* (animal). This refers to the nocturnal character of sorcerers and to their close association with animal familiars.

59.   Tauxier. *La Religion*, 160.

60.   Silla, Eric. *People Are Not the Same. Leprosy and Identity in Twentieth-Century Mali.* Portsmouth: Heinemann, 1998, 61.

61.   For further details on sorcery methods, see Imperato, Pascal James. *African Folk Medicine. Practices and Beliefs of the Bambara and Other Peoples.* Baltimore: York Press, 1977, 30–37; Tauxier. *La Religion*, 43–71, 245–263; and Henry. *L'Ame*, 151–153.

62.   Imperato. *African*, 36.

63.   *Boliw* have been documented and studied in the field by a number of observers during the twentieth century. For some earlier studies, see Henry. *L'Ame*, 133, 140–141, 151, and Monteil. *Les Bambara*, 253–257. More recent observations have been made by Brett-Smith. The Poisonous; Cissé, Youssouf Tata. *Boli*, Statues et statuettes dans la religion

Bambara. In *Magies* by Christiane Falgayrettes-Leveau, Suzanne Preston Blier, Youssouf Tata Cissé, Vincent Bouloré, and Arthur Bourgeois. Paris: Editions Dapper, 1996, 145–173; Colleyn and DeClippel. *Bamanaya*, 121–127; and McNaughton. *Secret*, 26–27. Colleyn and DeClippel provide some remarkable field photographs of *boliw* in situ in shrines and on display. While the word *boli* literally means "to run," "to flee," or "to carry away while running," its use to describe power objects derives from its other meanings which include "manifestation" and "emanation." See Bazin, *Dictionnaire*, 80; and Cissé, *Boli,* 145.

64.   Henry. *L'Ame*, 133.

65.   *Dassiriw* have been described by a number of observers. See especially Dieterlen. *Essai*, 137–139; Henry. *L'Ame*, 101–102; Imperato. *African*, 32–33; and Lem, F.H. Les Cultes des arbres et de génies protecteurs du sol au Soudan Français. *Bulletin de l'IFAN* 1948, 10:539–559.

66.   For details about various Bamana practitioners who deal with sorcery, see Imperato. *African*, 54–67; and Tauxier. *La Religion*, 220–244.

67.   Another term for the graphic signs on door locks is *nèguè misèn*, derived from the words *nèguè* (iron) and *misèn* (thin), no doubt referring to the thin, hot knife blade used for surface engraving. See Tesi. *Introduction*, 17. For an overview of graphic signs among the Bamana, Bozo, Dogon, and Keita, see Griaule, Marcel and Dieterlen, Germaine. *Signes graphiques Soudanais.* Paris: Hermann et Cie, 1951. The great planks (*walaw*) of the *Komo* carry the *ti baw* or great signs, also known as the mother signs. These are either pyroengraved or painted on the planks, and represent God's thoughts, and retrace the history of creation. For details concerning these planks, see Dieterlen and Cissé. *Les Fondements*, 41–42. The *karaw* (door mat) planks of the *Korè* society also bear pyroengraved and painted graphic signs used to teach and impart wisdom to initiates. The name of these planks is symbolic in that like rolled up door mats, they hide their interior (widsom), but reveal it when opened or exposed. For details, see Zahan. *Les Sociétés*, 143–149. Zahan uses the term *walaw* for these planks. This term is commonly applied to the small wooden writing tablets used by koranic students. The term for a large plank of wood such as that used on a house door is *dyiri fyèrè* (wood, cut up).

68.   Zahan, Dominique. Pictographic writing in the Western Sudan. *Man* 1950, 50:136–138. See also Griaule,

Marcel. Réflexions sur les symboles Soudanais. *Cahiers Internationaux de Sociologie* 1952; 13:8–30; de Ganay, Solange. Graphies Bambara des nombres. *Journal de la Société des Africanistes* 1950; 20:295–305; de Ganay, Solange. Aspects de mythologie et de symbolique Bambara. *Journal de Psychologie Normale et Pathologique* 1949, 42:181–201; de Ganay, Solange. Une graphie soudanaise du doit du Createur. *Revue de l'Histoire des Religions* 1951; 139:45–49; and de Ganay. II. Graphie.

69.   de Ganay. II. Graphie.

70.   Ibid.

71.   Ibid.

72.   In attempting to understand the meanings of graphic signs, one must remember the importance to the Bamana of controlled access to knowledge (and thus to power) based on age, gender, and *dyow* initiation. As a result, secrecy and ambiguity of meaning often guide spoken language. It frequently appears to outsiders that convoluted deductive reasoning is required to understand some spoken language and the meanings of graphic signs. Yet this type of reasoning is not difficult for the Bamana. They can easily decipher multiple and related meanings within the context of familiar logic and belief systems that deny effortless comprehension to the uninitiated.

73.   Zahan. Pictographic, 136.

74.   Dieterlen and Cissé. *Les Fondements*, 74.

75.   Ibid., 63.

76.   The X sign, known as *wolo ti* (birth sign), is closely associated with circumcision.

77.   For a fuller discussion of *bokolanfini* (*bogolanfini*), see Aherne, Tavey D. *Nakunte Diarra. Bogolanfini Artist of the Beledougou.* Bloomington: Indiana University Art Museum, 1992; Brett–Smith, Sarah C. Symbolic Blood. Cloths for Excised Women. *RES: Anthropology and Aesthetics* 1982, 3:15–31; and Imperato, Pascal James, and Shamir Marli. Bokolanfini. Mud Cloth of the Bamana of Mali. *African Arts* 1970; III(4):32–41, 80. For modern developments in the creation of this cloth, see Rovine, Victoria. *Bogolanfini* in Bamako. The Biography of a Malian Textile. *African Arts* 1997, XXX (1)40–51, 94–96.

PORTALS, DOORS, AND LOCKS

BAMANA VILLAGE ARCHITECTURE is dominated by extended family compounds (*douw*) (singular *dou*) which in turn are subdivided into individual family households known as *gouaw* (singular *goua*). In the eastern Bamana country, these architectural units are separated by mud brick walls five feet and higher in height and by the sides of buildings. In this same area, narrow common alleys traverse villages in a tortuous manner, and eventually lead in and out of them. While the same general architectural plan characterizes villages in the western Bamana country, there the houses are round with thatched roofs, and mud brick walls are less common. In the absence of the latter, the Bamana and Malinké use large screens or lattices made of vegetable fiber to set off areas of a *goua*. Many people in the western Bamana area have adopted rectangular house design and mud brick walls for segregating *douw* and *gouaw* from one another. These rectangular houses have either flat mud roofs or corrugated metal ones. The latter are usually set at an incline to allow for the runoff of rain water. The abandonment of conical thatched roofs has in part been driven by the greater permanency of their mud and metal counterparts and the increased difficulty in finding suitable replacement thatch.[1]

Illus. 36.
Extended family compounds (*douw*) in the eastern Bamana country separated by mud brick walls. Village of Boussin, Segou region (Cercle of Segou), 1969.

PORTALS AND DOORWAYS

Although the terms portal and doorway can be used synonymously, they are differentiated in this discussion to reflect subtleties in Bamana architecture. Both are known as *daw* (singular *da*) in *Bamanan-kan*. Portals are usually more elaborate and imposing entrances compared to simple doorways. This distinction is apparent in the architecture of many African peoples for whom portals represent major gateways to either towns or villages and their subdivisions. [2]

Portals and doorways have great symbolic significance for the Bamana. They represent familiar entrances through which people regularly pass in order to join their families and friends or to step out into the world beyond their village's walls. These entrances either give or deny access to strangers, and can be secured at night to keep harmful individuals, forces, and spirits out.

The principal entrance to some Bamana villages consists of an elaborate portal constructed of mud brick whose lintel

Illus. 37.
Family compound (*goua*) in the western Bamana country separated by vegetable fiber screens. The exteriors of some houses are decorated with kaolin designs.
Village of Tiebasa, Fouladougou Arbala region (Cercle of Kita), 1969.

(*dankoun*) supports either a simple or elaborate superstructure.[3] This type of portal is known as "portal of the ancestors" (*folo maou dou da* or *gale maou dou da*).[4] Imposing portals of this type project a visual image of power and strength that impresses strangers and reassures local villagers. While some of these portals constitute a simple gateway, others lead into a large vestibule (*blo*) which has an opening on the other side that gives access to the village.

The Bamana place *boliw* in these vestibules, usually above the lintel (*dankoun*) of the principal exterior doorway. Sacrifices are periodically made to these *boliw* both to invoke the help and protection of village ancestors, and to prevent nefarious *nyama* and spirits and malevolent individuals from crossing the threshold of the portal. Sacrifices to ancestors are placed on the external walls of these portals often consisting of the blood and feathers of a white chicken mixed with millet gruel.[5]

When ancestral portals are originally constructed, protective *boliw*, plants, and talismans are placed in terra cotta pots and buried beneath the thresholds (*binakounw*).[6] This practice is also followed with the construction of *blow*, the objects being placed beneath the thresholds of both doorways. The burying of protective *boliw*, talismans, and herbs in terra cotta pots beneath thresholds is still practiced in some areas of the

Illus. 38.
The *Kamablo* sanctuary, gateway to the Mande world.
Village of Kangaba, Mande region
(Cercle of Kangaba), 1967.

PORTALS, DOORS, AND LOCKS

Bamana country when a new dwelling is built.[7] Paques recorded this tradition among the southern Bamana in the middle of the twentieth century. She also noted that protective herbal preparations were buried beneath the outer layer of mud stucco to the right of the doorway in order to assure the fertility of the woman who would occupy the house.[8]

Illus. 39.
Ancestral portal (*folo maou dou da*) for the village of Sogonafing, Djitoumou region (Cercle of Bamako), 1971.

Village portals symbolically and physically separate human habitation from the wild world of the bush and field beyond. This world is especially dangerous at night because the Bamana believe that is the time it is frequented by nefarious *nyama*, sorcerers, thieves, and malevolent people and spirits. The Bamana refer to this dark and dangerous nightly world as *dibi*. This word incorporates not only the idea of darkness and night, but also that of extreme danger, and is applied to those places that lie beyond the confines of villages.[9]

The portal to an extended family's compound (*dou*) usually consists of a large room-like vestibule (*blo*) containing two directly opposite doorways (*daw*). In the western Bamana country, the vestibule can be a standard round house with a thatched roof, while in the eastern area it usually consists of a rectangular-shaped mud brick room. Both types of vestibules have a doorway facing the outside, and one directly opposite leading to the compound. Doors, when they are present, are most often hung in the outer doorway and secured by an internal lock mounted on a post. Thus, the door can be secured at night from the inside. Visiting strangers are usually permitted to sleep in a family's *blo*, and the men of an extended family often use it as a meeting place. Domestic animals such as goats and sheep are sometimes housed there as well.

Illus. 40.
The center of a family compound (*goua*). Village of Sirakoro, Djitoumou region (Cercle of Bamako), 1970. (Photograph by Marli Shamir).

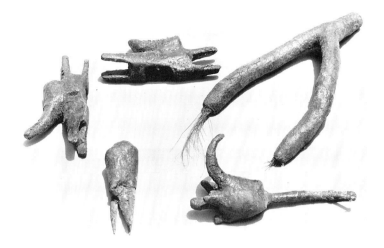

Illus. 41.
Boliw of the *Komo* society collected by the author in Mali in 1968 (Photograph by Marli Shamir).

Boliw are frequently placed above the lintel of the doorway of a vestibule leading to the exterior. In addition, protective *boliw* and talismans are buried in terra cotta pots beneath the threshold, and sacrificial offerings of millet and white chicken feathers and blood placed on the exterior walls of the doorway. Sacrificial materials comprised of animal dung, blood, and millet porridge are sometimes smeared on the external surfaces of a vestibule door, especially on the center and the left side, which are routinely touched in the process of pushing it inward from the outside. Such sacrificial materials are believed capable of thwarting sorcerers, nefarious *nyama*, and malevolent people

and spirits.[10] Over time, an encrustation is built up on the left side of the door, especially on the edge, which also becomes highly patinated through routine use.

The only doorways inside of a village are those to individual dwellings, kitchens, and other structures such as granaries. *Boliw* are often interred in terra cotta pots beneath the thresholds of dwellings, talismans sealed beneath the mud stucco next to the doorways, and *boliw* placed above the lintels.

For the Bamana, portals and doorways are necessary architectural structures that provide access to villages and their dwellings. Yet these openings paradoxically constitute a continual danger. For it is through them that a variety of malevolent beings, forces, and spirits can enter a village or home and cause harm. In order to meet this challenge, the Bamana have endowed these openings with architectural forms that usually project a sense of power and accretions such as *boliw*, talismans, and sacrifices that invoke the protection of ancestors and other spiritual forces. The presence of these objects above lintels, below thresholds, and along the sides of portals and doorways speaks of a comprehensive effort to reduce the risks associated with an open entrance. Doors that close the openings of vestibules and houses, and the sculpted locks that secure them, form part of this effort. These doors do not merely act as physical impediments to unwanted visitors because they are also endowed with protective spiritual powers through the sacrificial materials that are sometimes smeared on their external surfaces.[11] These powers are augmented by those of sculpted locks whose architectonics represent even greater spiritual forces.

Illus. 42.
Palaver scaffolding (*goua* or *gouala*) reserved for men. Village of Boussin, Segou region (Cercle of Segou), 1969.

PORTALS, DOORS, AND LOCKS

DOORS

The Bamana view doors and locks not only as functional objects, but also as spiritual ones that form part of their comprehensive effort to control sorcery and other malevolent forces and beings. Therefore, these objects should be understood within the broad context of their relationship to portals and doorways and other spiritual and philosophical dimensions of *Bamanaya*.

The Bamana believe that the first spoken word was *kon* (door), and that it has enormous power because it protects from all forms of intrusion. It symbolizes not merely a physical barrier to the outside world, but also one to a person's internal thoughts, because thoughts and knowledge expressed as words can reveal either strength or weakness. Thus, silence and secrecy are important intellectual doors which should be opened only after careful reflection and when appropriate. They are the doors to inner thoughts which can only be revealed if an individual so wishes. They enable people to hide their thoughts and knowledge from others, much as a door bars the view of a house's interior from passersby.

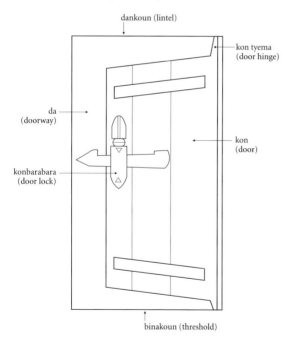

dankoun (lintel)

kon tyema
(door hinge)

da
(doorway)

kon
(door)

konbarabara
(door lock)

binakoun (threshold)

Illus. 43.
Components of a Bamana doorway and door.

Doors also represent tranquility because of their association with the concept of silence. For the Bamana, silence is the key to peace of mind because it helps them avoid the conflict and controversy that frequently emanate from spoken words. The Bamana give emphasis to this belief through the use of several aphorisms such as, *Dade hakili sigime, kuma hakili*

wilime. Literally translated, this means, "Silence has a tranquil mind, speech an agitated one."[12]

When the Bamana say that silence represents perfection in communication, they mean that it is a very important characteristic of speech. Like a door, it can be used at will to either expose or hide what is within. Silence emphasizes words that have just been spoken and those that follow. In a sense, it speaks powerfully in the absence of words. Those who punctuate their speech with silence also carefully choose their words. Thus, silence gives greater weight to what is spoken and speaks for what is not said. Those who use it well demonstrate discretion, patience, self-control, wisdom, and power.

Bamana doors are used in a variety of doorways including houses (external and internal), vestibules, sanctuaries, granaries, kitchens, and poultry shelters. They are often equipped with sculpted locks, though doors on *Komo* and other sanctuaries usually lack them. Doors are hewn from local woods by blacksmiths using adzes of which there are several types.[13] Doors are comprised of from two to five planks or panels known as *dyiri fyèrèw* (singular *dyiri fyèrè*). This term derives from the *Bamanan-kan* words *dyiri* (wood) and *fyèrè* (cut up). Blacksmiths prefer sturdy woods for the panels of doors such as *Ficus capensis*, known as *toro* in *Bamanan-kan* and *Khaya senegalensis* (*dala*). If these woods are not available, others are used. Panels produced in sawmills in the Ivory Coast occasionally have been crafted into doors. However, industrially produced boards have long been used by the Songhay of Timbuctoo for making doors.[14]

Illus. 44.
Three-paneled house door with lock depicting a stylized *bamada* hat.
Village of Sirakoro, Djitoumou region (Cercle of Bamako), 1969.
(Photograph by Marli Shamir).

Doors are made to order because blacksmiths must craft them to fit doorways of varying dimensions. What is particularly critical is a good fit for the hinges (*kon tyemaw*). This term derives from the noun *kon* (door) and the adjective *tyema* (masculine), and is an obvious allusion to the penile character of hinges. Even though blacksmiths measure doorways before crafting doors, the fit is not always perfect. Thus, one finds spaces between the lintel and the top of the door, and between the threshold and the bottom of it. Such spaces also develop over time as people modify the lintels and thresholds. Thresholds are often elevated above the level of the ground and the floor of the house in order to prevent the entry of water during the rainy season. While the fit of a door may not be precise in terms of height, it is almost invariably so with regard to width because otherwise the lock would not function properly.

In the past, house doors and locks figured prominently in Bamana marriage customs. A door with an attached lock was sometimes given to a daughter just before she left home to reside permanently in the new house built for her by her husband. The young woman and her entourage of relatives and friends would carry the door and lock along with pots, pans, other utensils, and clothing to the husband's village where the door was hung in the doorway of her new home. This practice was described to me in detail by the late Modjie Samaké of the village of Senou, one of whose grandsons, Amadou Coulibaly, worked with me as a vaccinator. She was born in 1878 in the village of Zougoumé, which is in the Arrondissement of Sanankoroba (Cercle of Bamako). In 1896, when she was eighteen years old, she was married to Tyéblé Coulibaly of Senou who was then twenty-six years old, having been born in 1870.

She was his first wife, and arrived in Senou with a door and lock that had been sculpted in Zougoumé at her parents' request (Illustration 45). The blacksmith who sculpted both the door and lock had previously traveled to Senou to verify the dimensions of the house Tyéblé Coulibaly had recently built for her.

Tyéblé Coulibaly died in 1948 at the age of seventy-eight. As a widow, Modjie Samaké continued to live in the round house with a thatched roof that he had originally built for her in 1896. Periodically refurbished with new thatch and stucco, it was still intact in 1969 when I first met her. Her marriage door and lock were also in use. [15]

Another practice was for a young bride to arrive in her husband's village with a door only.[16] The lock, made by the same or another blacksmith, was then given to her by her husband as a sign of affection and esteem, and affixed to the door. A third practice was for a husband to give a lock to his wife only after she had given birth to a male child. The giving of the lock and its attachment to the door occurred simultaneously with the placement of three stones in the *goua*, symbolizing the permanency of the marriage as well as the husband, wife, and their son.[17]

While Bamana house doors vary in height from 50 to 60 inches, their widths are generally within a narrower spectrum of 25 to 27 inches. This reflects a Bamana practice of configuring house doorways so that their heights are roughly twice their widths. The dimensions of doors for kitchens are roughly the same. However, those for other types of openings vary considerably. Double doors were not traditionally used by the Bamana, though they are encountered today on some modern buildings. Such doors are invariably made of metal or corrugated metal sheets laid over wooden frames.

Illus. 45.
Door lock depicting a highly stylized *bamada* hat sculpted for Modjie Samaké in 1896 at the time of her marriage to Tyéblé Coulibaly.
Village of Senou, Djitoumou region (Cercle of Bamako), 1968.

Illus. 46.
Extremely old house door with a lock representing the *koro* lizard and a modern padlock. The metal key is inserted into the superior open end of the horizontal beam.
Village of Senou, Djitoumou region (Cercle of Bamako), 1971.

PORTALS, DOORS, AND LOCKS

The panels of a door are held together by metal dowels that are inserted into their inner side surfaces. These are substantial in size, and on older doors are made of indigenously forged metal. They are generally inserted a few inches from the tops and bottoms of the panels. Fixation of the panels to one another is further achieved by the use of wooden crossbars placed across the upper and lower portions of a door a few inches from the ends. These crossbars are often attached by indigenously smelted nails, though in recent decades, industrial ones have also been used. Blacksmiths sometimes scallop or bevel the edges of these crossbars or modify their form in order to make them more attractive. Panel attachment is sometimes further achieved through the use of U-shaped metal brackets that may be placed on either the inside or outside of the door.

weight, and thus wore down at a faster rate than the upper ones. Not infrequently, the lower hinge wears out altogether and is replaced by a new one that is affixed by nails to the posterior lower end of the right-sided panel. How hinges wear is very much determined by how a door is hung. This has varied over time, and has been influenced by the availability of newer materials.

Hinges are often simply inserted into matching holes in the rear part of the masonry lintel and threshold. Sometimes strips of wood are placed over these or portions of them, and holes made to accommodate the hinges. In recent decades, inverted thick glass bottles have been buried in the masonry of thresholds to serve as the principal support for the lower hinges of doors. Another method of lower hinge mounting is the creation of a mound of masonry on the house floor just behind the threshold. The lower hinge is then inserted into a hole in this masonry mound.

Illus. 47.
House door with lock depicting a stylized *bamada* hat temporarily removed from mounting for doorway masonry repair. The upper and lower hinges are clearly visible. Village of Kologo, Bougouni region (Cercle of Bougouni), 1973.

Door hinges are usually carved at the upper and lower lateral edge of the right-sided panel.[18] They are roughly cylindrical in shape, and measure anywhere from two to five inches in length. The hinges on doors in Western collections are often unequal in length because the lower ones bore more of the

Illus. 48.
Door with a sculpted lock mounted on a poultry shelter. Village of Kodiala, Fouladougou Arbala region (Cercle of Kita), 1970.

34

LOCKS

Bamana wooden house doors usually open toward the inside. Exceptions to this rule include the doors for granaries and poultry shelters, which open to the outside and which usually have right-sided hinges. Many modern doors constructed of wooden frames covered with corrugated metal sheeting open to the outside.

The patina on doors tends to be most prominent on those surface areas most frequently touched during routine use. These include the top, the left and right edges, and the mid-portion of the left and middle panels, especially around the wooden lock. On some very old doors, this patina has an encrustation quality, due to the accumulation of dirt and food residues over many years. However, some areas of encrustation on doors, especially those over the center, are due to sacrificial materials consisting of millet porridge, dung, and chicken blood.

While their close neighbors, the Dogon and Senufo, sculpt the exterior surfaces of doors, this practice is rare among the Bamana. While visiting hundreds of Bamana villages over a 5-year period in the late 1960s and early 1970s, this writer observed only one sculpted door in situ.[19] A small number of Bamana doors with sculpted surfaces have been exhibited and some have been illustrated or described in Western publications, and one is depicted in the Catalogue section of this book (Figure 57). However, locks have frequently been exhibited and illustrated in publications.[20]

During the last few decades of the twentieth century, several factors led to the gradual abandonment of wooden door use. Among them was the relatively higher cost of a new wooden door compared to a corrugated metal one, the inability of blacksmiths to find trees of sufficient diameter to cut the necessary planks, and the association of wooden doors and their sculpted locks with an ancestral religion, many of whose beliefs have been abandoned by a majority of the population.

Bamana door locks are remarkable wooden sculptures that incorporate complex symbols and architectonics which reflect the spiritual and philosophical beliefs of *Bamanaya*. They were once extremely common in most Bamana villages, but during the latter decades of the twentieth century, they were progressively discarded, and few new ones were made by blacksmiths.[21]

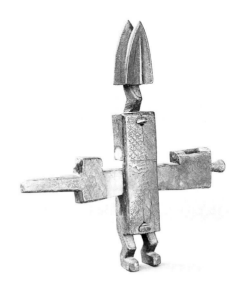

Illus. 49.
Bamana lock depicting a stylized *bamada* hat and the open jaws of the crocodile. Djitoumou region (Cercle of Bamako). (Photograph taken in Mali by the late Eliot Elisofon, 1970. Courtesy of the National Museum of African Art, Smithsonian Institution, Eliot Elisofon Photographic Archives). See also Figure 8 in the Catalogue section.

The Recent History of Locks

Informants give several reasons for the disappearance of sculpted door locks. Most frequently, they say, "People began to pray," meaning that they embraced Islam, and thus discarded the material representations of *Bamanaya*. There is much truth in this, but there were other forces at work as well. Following World War II, many Malian men returned from military service in Europe. These *anciens combattants* (veterans) introduced the use of modern metal locks on a large scale, especially in the cercles of Bamako and Bougouni from where many men had been recruited.[22] Their service during the war also eroded their ties to *Bamanaya*, giving further impetus to the discarding of sculpted locks. Around the same time, a fundamentalist anti-Sufi Islamic movement, the *Wahabiya*, was introduced from Saudi Arabia with pilgrims returning from the *haj* (pilgrimage to Mecca). It rapidly spread in the western Bamana area, especially among traders in the cercles of Bamako and Bougouni.[23] The *Wahabi*, as the followers of this movement are known, avidly destroyed the external manifestations of *Bamanaya*, including the removal of door locks.

Because they were traders, they also created a market for these old locks among Europeans living in Bamako, the capital of the then French Sudan (now Mali).[24] The erosion of *Bamanaya*, coupled with a market for old locks, accelerated their removal. Many recent converts to Islam, wishing to give public proof of their orthodoxy, removed their old locks, but sometimes allowed them to rot in a corner of the family compound, fearful of the consequences of allowing their *nyama* to escape. This problem was often dealt with by calling in a Moslem cleric (*imam*) whose powers were capable of handling a lock's *nyama*. These clerics either burned locks, along with masks and *boliw*, threw them into the hollows of large baobab trees where they eventually rotted, or else sold them to the agents of Bamako-based art traders.[25]

It was not uncommon for an owner to return the lock to the blacksmith who sculpted it, if he were still alive. The same was done with some other forms of sculpture such as masks and marionettes. For these smiths, as the original creators of the objects, were believed best able to handle their *nyama* and to prevent adverse consequences befalling those who had discarded them. Blacksmiths either stored the objects or sold them to the agents of Bamako's art dealers, whose numbers greatly increased beginning in the 1960s.[26]

It is of note that the greatest diversity in lock form during the twentieth century was found in the western and southern Bamana areas, which were then far less influenced by Islam than was their eastern counterpart. In the east, and especially around Segou, the capital of the old Bamana kingdom, the simple iguana form predominated. This may have been the result of the Moslem Tukulor conquest of this area in 1861. As members of the *Tidjaniya* Sufi order, the Tukulor were intolerant of representational art forms, but valued the iconography of the iguana.[27] Bamana, wishing to avoid the wrath of these militant Moslems when they were in power, would have been inclined to remove sculpted door locks depicting forms other than the iguana because they were permanent public declarations of adherence to *Bamanaya*. Masks and *boliw*, on the other hand, could be hidden from Tukulor inspection for long periods of time.[28]

The Tukulor, who ruled much of the eastern Bamana area from 1861 through 1890, after which they were driven out by the French, took every opportunity to destroy the material representations of *Bamanaya* and to severely punish those who possessed them. Tauxier vividly recounts two anecdotes describing how the Tukulor dealt with the *Komo*. On one occasion, a group of Tukulor calvary arrived in a village that was observing the periodic appearance of two *Komo* masqueraders. As the large crowd of spectators fled, the Tukulor threatened to set fire to the straw and cloth armatures worn by the two men. Although the two masqueraders pleaded for their lives, they were sold into slavery that day at a nearby market. In another instance, a Tukulor was visiting a village when the *Komo* masquerader emerged at night. The Tukulor immediately set fire to the armature and broke the masquerader's legs. The villagers did not come to the aid of the masquerader, fearful that if they did, a column of Tukulor soldiers would be sent to destroy the village.[29]

Despite these pressures, large numbers of Bamana, especially in the western and southern areas, retained their sculpted locks, either because they still adhered to *Bamanaya* or because they embraced a less militant form of Islam in which syncretism was possible. Although people held on to their locks, few new ones were made after the 1940s. This was due to the reduced vibrancy of *Bamanaya* in many areas, and the fact that blacksmiths found more lucrative and easier incomes making and repairing farm implements for an expanding modern agricultural economy.[30] In the transition from *Bamanaya* to Islam, it was relatively easy to be considered a good Moslem while still retaining an old lock, given its powerful *nyama* and connections to ancestors. On the other hand, ordering a new lock and attaching it to a door would have represented a very public declaration of adherence to *Bamanaya*. No recent adherent to Islam would have considered such a course of action, if for no other reason than that of jeopardizing their newly acquired social status in a community undergoing progressive Islamization.

Illus. 50. Four-paneled door with a lock depicting the rudimentary form of a lizard often found in the late twentieth century in the eastern Bamana country. The lock is mounted on the right, and the horizontal beam turned inside out, two unusual characteristics. Village of Ngoloba, Segou region (Cercle of Segou), 1974.

Illus. 51.
The late Bakary Coulibaly with a four-paneled door and lock given to his wife at the time of their marriage in the early 1920s. The lock is sculpted in the rudimentary form of a reptile, then common in the eastern Bamana country. Three panels of the door have been reinforced by a wooden plank. Village of Sie, Segou region (Cercle of San), 1973.

Overall, the sculpting of wooden door locks among the Bamana has been on the wane for many decades. Not many are being sculpted today, given the decline of *Bamanaya*, and the availability of alternative materials for doors and the wide availability of modern locks.

One should not underestimate the eventual destructive effects of Islam on indigenous Bamana culture based on initial syncretism and early accommodative gestures. Over the long term, Islam has not shown itself to be accommodating to most of the essential beliefs of traditional religions nor tolerant of their religious representational art. Vivid testimony of this is given by Yaya Diallo, a Minianka artist who now lives in Kentucky. In his book, *The Healing Drum*, he states the following.[31]

Islam causes me more fear for my endangered culture. I find it is possible to be in dialogue with people from the West, but conversion to Islam requires rejection of traditional beliefs and practices. People of my tribe who became Moslems had to kill what was African in themselves. In one day, they learned their prayers and were instructed to burn their drums and masks.

I am not certain that the sort of conversion practiced in Mali can make good Moslems out of people, as it happens so quickly. The repetition of prayer five times daily requires some discipline but does not make serious demands on people to understand. Yet the promise of an afterlife is very inviting.

Diallo, a traditionalist who was reared adhering to Minianka beliefs and practices, which are similar to some of those of the Bamana, describes not a gradual process of Islamization, but a rapid one pushed forward through intimidation and the instillation of fear.

One of the popular methods in Mali of proselytizing for Islam involves distributing booklets profusely illustrated with pictures of people who are in hell for engaging in actions contrary to Islamic teachings. The pictures are persuasive and instill much fear.

Another disturbing feature of the spread of Islam is the way the proselytizers take advantage of some of the fundamental values of our culture to undermine it. To our old people, for example, a proper burial and funeral are very important. At times, some of the younger generation convert to Islam first and then tell the elders that they will not touch the corpses of heathen. The elders, for fear of not being decently buried, begin to say their Moslem prayers.

This rare account by an African traditionalist provides excellent documentation that the adoption of Islam can at times be rapid and devastating to traditional customs and their material expressions. It also makes clear that attempts by Western researchers to reconstruct the details of a pre-Islamic *Bamanaya* past can meet with great obstacles. For the revelation of this past comes into sharp conflict with a population's concerted attempts to reinvent itself and revise its own history within an Islamic context.

Not surprisingly then, I encountered considerable difficulty in some locations in trying to reconstruct the history of lock sculpting, especially where the population had converted to Islam. Some individuals exhibited selective amnesia about the history of extant locks, and about the blacksmiths who had sculpted them. The fact that a number of blacksmiths had either moved away or abandoned their profession for other types of work often made it difficult for me to establish which of their families had contributed to making an area a center of lock-sculpting excellence.

The desire to be seen not only as a Moslem, but also as a member of a village Islamic tradition extending far back into time, frequently results in total disavowal of any knowledge of the recent *Bamanaya* past. The Islamic historical tradition is then either explicitly stated or inferred, but in either case, often invented. During my field research, I encountered blacksmiths who were unwilling to identify those ancestors who had created magnificent sculptures, some of which were still in place. The continued presence of locks on doors would seem to present a contradiction to claims of an ancient adherence to Islam. However, informants dealt with this issue by simply ascribing great age to them, extending back before many generations of followers of Islam.

While some blacksmiths demonstrated a reticence to associate themselves and their families with sculpted locks, they were more willing to do so with entertainment-type masks. For locks are religious objects embodying much of the essence of *Bamanaya*, while entertainment masks and masquerades are playthings (*tulonkèfenw*). These considerations may well have been the reason why Kéléya blacksmiths refused to reveal much information about locks to Tesi in 1971. As a result, her interpreter, Wa Kamisoko, who was a bard (*dyeli*), had to obtain much of the information she was seeking.

Illus. 52.
Lock representing *Mouso Koroni Koundyé.*
Village of Faladie, Bélédougou region (Cercle of Kolokani), 1971.

The inability to attribute given works of African art to specific artists is often lamented in the West. Yet, as described above, some attempts to do so in the field in Africa are often thwarted by Africans themselves. In the case of some Bamana recently converted to Islam, it is a changed religious and cultural context that induces them to impose anonymity on the authors of great religious works of art of the *Bamanaya* era. In time, and over the span of one or two generations following conversion to Islam, this *Bamanaya* heritage, along with its heros and great people, is easily forgotten, or else recast in a mythologized Islamic historical fiction.

Centers of Lock-Sculpting Excellence

On examining locks both in Western collections and in situ, it becomes clear that there were centers where blacksmiths excelled at sculpting these objects. To this evidence can be added local oral historical accounts which often are specific as to villages and even blacksmith families. Yet, there are limitations to these streams of evidence. The precise origins of locks in collections are often not known, or else are not reliable. The earliest made locks found in collections do not date to earlier than the beginning of the nineteenth century. Most date to a much later period. Thus, the corpus of locks extant outside of Mali provides a retrospective view on possible centers of sculptural excellence that reaches back only a century and a half.

Illus. 53.
Lock depicting the *koro* lizard with its metal key resting in the superior opening of the horizontal beam.
Village of Sirakoro, Djitoumou region (Cercle of Bamako), 1970. (Photograph by Marli Shamir).

The absence of a firm historical record in the form of locks sculpted earlier than the nineteenth century limits our ability to identify centers of excellence to only a limited period of time. The oral historical record is of little help overall for the period before this because of the knowledge loss inherent in generation transfer of information and re-invention and revision under the influence of Islam.

Despite these limitations, however, it is clear that several centers of lock sculpting existed in the nineteenth and twentieth centuries. Blacksmiths in these areas not only sculpted a rich diversity of forms, but were also superb artists who produced great works of art. These centers were primarily located in the western part of the Bamana country extending in the south from Bougouni through Banimounitie and Djitoumou, to Bélédougou in the north. Within this vast area, the blacksmiths of Bougouni enjoyed a reputation as the best sculptors of locks. Even within Bougouni, villages such as Kéléya were home to blacksmiths renowned as far to the east as Segou for their skills at sculpting locks.

Illus. 54.
Two-paneled house door and a lock whose symbolism is obscure. Village of Niosombougou, Bélédougou region (Cercle of Kolokani), 1970.

These centers of sculpting excellence arose because of the vibrancy of *Bamanaya* and the presence of lineages of skilled master sculptor-blacksmiths. They were sustained by the same two variables, but began to decline as *Bamanaya* progressively lost ground to the advance of Islam.

The Sculpting of Locks

The Bamana employ a variety of terms for door locks, the most common one being *konbarabara* (door, protuberance). The word *bara* has several other meanings among which are "gourd" and "to surprise." Other terms used for door locks include *kon-soua-balabala* (door, lock, protuberance), and *kon-goussana* (door, home, passage).[32]

Illus. 55.
Two-paneled granary door and a lock whose serrated neck represents the tail of the large black scorpion (*dyonkomi*). This recalls the wretched life and death of *Mouso Koroni Koundyé*. Village of Bouala, Bélédougou region (Cercle of Kolokani), 1970. See also Figure 14 in the Catalogue section.

The mechanical principles of Bamana locks have been attributed by various writers to Egypt, Sumer, Babylon, and the Roman Empire. Their diffusion from North Africa into the Western Sudan is thought to have been facilitated by Islam. Similar locks were still in use in North Africa in the twentieth century, though devoid of representational art. Even if the Bamana adopted the basic mechanics of an ancient lock form, they surrounded them with unique and complex sculptures reflecting their own religious and philosophical beliefs. In so doing, they also created magnificent works of art. [33]

The architectonics and mechanics of Bamana locks are similar to those used by the Bwa, Dogon, Malinké, Mossi, and Senufo. Dogon locks, especially the larger ones used on house doors, are sometimes confused with Bamana locks. Stylistic considerations aside, these locks can be distinguished from one another by a number of structural features. Dogon house door locks are usually wider than those of the Bamana, often by a third, but are only half as deep. The locking pins in Dogon locks are smaller in diameter, often by a half. The key insertion in Dogon locks is invariably lateral, and the keys are almost always comprised of a wooden shaft with metal teeth at one end. As in Bamana locks, the teeth are embedded perpendicularly on one side of the shaft. Like the Bamana, the Dogon also use post locks (*dur kunu*) that are mounted on the inside of rooms. [34]

Sculpted of wood, Bamana locks consist of two parts, a vertical beam and a horizontal one (the bolt). The former ranges in length from ten to forty inches, with the average being sixteen inches. The horizontal beam varies in length from ten to eighteen inches, but on average is fourteen to fifteen inches long. Although horizontal beams are not always proportional to the vertical ones, they are usually slightly shorter. It is extremely rare for a horizontal beam to be longer than its vertical counterpart. Consequently, the overall form of a given lock is an extremely balanced one. The keys for locks are made either entirely of metal or consist of a wooden rod with metal teeth at one end. Keys average eight inches in length, but can be longer or shorter.

In the past, locks were frequently sculpted for women at the time they left their parents' home to join their new husbands. They were also given to women by their husbands as a sign of esteem and affection once they had given birth to a son. As such, they conferred enhanced social status on a woman within her husband's extended family and the larger village community. This association of locks with marriage and with women who have given birth to sons leads many Bamana to view them as feminine objects. They are so viewed even when attached to the doors of men's houses (*tye sow*), rooms where husbands meet and entertain friends. The Bamana reason that such locks, which are usually commissioned by wives and given as gifts to their husbands, act as surveillance agents for the former. As a result, they retain a feminine quality. [35]

Illus. 56.
Two-paneled granary door with a lock depicting the rudimentary form of a reptile. A modern padlock is also attached to the door. Village of Samantara, Bélédougou region (Cercle of Kolokani), 1970.

Locks are sculpted by blacksmiths only when requested by a client. They are never sculpted and placed on sale at a weekly market as is the case with some Dogon locks.[36] Because locks are subjected to the wear inherent in continuous use, they are usually sculpted from some of the same hard woods that are used for constructing doors.[37] These woods include *Ficus capensis* (*toro*), *Khaya senegalensis* (*dala*), the caicedrat tree, *Diospyros mespiliformis* (*sunsun*), *Lannea acida* (*bémbé*), and *Cola cordifolia* (*ntaba*). Blacksmiths express a preference for the wood of the *toro* tree because of its durability. [38] However, tree scarcity often forces compromise choices. This has especially been true since the middle of the twentieth century due to the degradation of savanna from droughts and shifting patterns of cultivation.

The cutting of a tree is fraught with great danger for a blacksmith because of its *nyama*. Therefore, a number of rituals are performed before it is cut in order to both appease and neutralize the spirit of the tree.[39] Blacksmiths sculpt locks in their forges, which are often located in their family compounds (*douw*). However, smiths can be itinerant, and in these instances they set up their forges in distant villages. This itinerancy is the result of a need to travel to where there is a demand for work such as repairing or creating farm and other implements. A blacksmith can begin to sculpt an object in one forge, and complete it in another. In 1970, I ordered a pair of *Tyi Wara* antelope head-dresses from Bafing Kané, who was a master sculptor-blacksmith in the village of Koké in the Arrondissement of Markala, Cercle of Segou. Because I was studying the sculpturing of these objects, I regularly visited his forge as the work progressed. One day, he told me that he had to move to the nearby village of Biawéré to make farm implements. He took the partially completed headdresses with him to this village, where he continued to sculpt them. He finished when he returned to Koké a few weeks later. Kané traveled as far away as the Cercle of Koutiala in the Minianka country, where he sculpted masks and made and repaired farm implements.[40]

Illus. 57.
The late Bafing Kané, a master sculptor-blacksmith, sculpting a *Tyi Wara* antelope headdress. Early in his career, he had sculpted door locks, but had not done so for over two decades. Village of Koké, Segou region (Cercle of Segou), 1970.

The sculpting of a lock begins with the vertical beam. This is the portion of a lock that can portray a wide range of human, animal, and abstract forms. The decision as to which form is sculpted is one that is made by a client after consultation with a blacksmith. However, because certain blacksmiths enjoy reputations as being skilled in creating given forms, clients may specifically seek them out on this account. Artistic skill is both locally and regionally recognized. Thus, a client may travel to a distant village to order a lock from a blacksmith known to create a certain form of high artistic quality.

Blacksmiths use several types of adzes in sculpting the vertical beam.[41] Once the general form of the vertical beam is achieved, the blacksmith turns his attention to its posterior surface, which must be flattened in order to achieve snug fixation to a door. More importantly, he must carve out a large rectangular cavity that will accommodate the sliding horizontal beam, and superior to this a much smaller recess that will contain the locking pins. In order to determine the size of this posterior cavity, the blacksmith must rough out the horizontal beam to be sure that it will fit into the cavity. Thus, while both beams are still in rough form, the artist concentrates on the mechanics of the locking system.

Illus. 58.
Three-paneled interior door and lock in the home of Siriman Fané, a master sculptor-blacksmith who sculpted them in the 1930s. A modern padlock is also attached to a chain. Siriman said that the lock represented a crocodile, a powerful anti-sorcery image. Village of Koké, Segou region (Cercle of Segou), 1971.

The horizontal beam (bolt) consists of five distinct portions. Beginning on the left is a tapered bar that fits into the masonry hole of the doorway. This portion is sculpted first, and those to the right of it sequentially afterwards. Next come lips or catches sculpted as part of the superior, inferior or both borders of the beam. These prevent the beam from completely sliding out of the cavity in the vertical beam when pulled to the right or pushed to the left. These are very often on the superior border, though it is not unusual for them to be on both borders. Even when they are sculpted only as part of the superior one, blacksmiths usually broaden the inferior border just opposite so that it too represents an impediment to the beam sliding out of its recess. On a lock that has a rectangular superior key insertion configuration, it serves as the lip to prevent the beam from sliding too far to the left. Rarely, a horizontal beam does not have a well-defined left lip. In such instances, a catch is created by a broadening of the beam, either superiorly or inferiorly, just before the beginning of its tapered end (Figures 33 and 40 in the Catalogue section). As the blacksmith is sculpting the horizontal beam, from left to right, he must know which type of key insertion he plans to create. There are only two types on Bamana locks, and both are at the right end of the horizontal beam. The key can either be inserted at the lateral end of the beam or through an elevated rectangular opening on the superior border. The lateral insertion usually requires a wooden key equipped with metal teeth at its distal end, whereas an all-metal key is used with the superior approach.

Illus. 59.
Close-up of lock depicted in Illus. 58, mounted on a door separating Siriman's bedroom from his storeroom.
Village of Koké, Segou region (Cercle of Segou), 1971.

Once the blacksmith has carved the horizontal beam with all of its external characteristics, including a tapered end, lips, and key insertion configuration, he is ready to begin the task of creating the locking mechanism. Both Moussa Coulibaly and Siriman Fané, master sculptor-blacksmiths from the eastern Bamana area, and Makan Fané, a master sculptor-blacksmith from Bélédougou, always began this process by hollowing out a large canal in the posterior surface of the horizontal beam. This canal roughly extends from the key insertion area for a third or a half of the length of the beam. It terminates just beyond the locking holes that are on the superior edge of this beam.

In order to achieve a precise locking device, the blacksmith first creates the key. Keys are equipped with anywhere from one to five teeth, with two being the average. Keys intended for lateral insertion are actually sculpted wooden sticks with metal teeth inserted at right angles to their terminal anterior surfaces. Metal keys are used for the more complex superior insertion. These keys are forged with long handles, which are then bent downward at a right angle. A second upward bend creates an elbow, after which comes a length of metal on which the teeth are created. The most distal tooth is often made by simply bending the very end of the key upward at a right angle. The one behind it is sometimes created by bending the thickened distal portion of the metal upward off the base of the rod. The teeth on metal keys are usually linear in their spatial relationships. There can be from one to three teeth on such keys, but two is usual. It would be difficult for such keys to have more than three teeth, given the narrow superior introitus through which they must pass. The teeth on wooden keys are often linear with regard to one another, but when there are more than two teeth, the width of the wooden stick often permits different spatial relationships.

Illus. 60.
The late Moussa Coulibaly, a master sculptor-blacksmith from the eastern Bamana country blackening the surface of a recently sculpted N'Tomo mask with a hot spatula. At the time, he had not sculpted door locks in many years.
Village of Touganabougou, Segou region (Cercle of Segou), 1973.

In the early part of the twentieth century, the metal for keys and locking pins was often forged from locally extracted iron ore. However, by the end of that century, most metal was derived from scrap objects such as the springs of trucks and cars which were sometimes forged into swords. In the late 1960s, I visited two separate locations where iron ore was still being extracted and smelted in large conical furnaces. One of these was a Minianka village in the Arrondissement of Kimparana, Cercle of San, and the other was a Bamana village in the Arrondissement of Bla, Cercle of Koutiala. Both areas had rich iron ore deposits, and this, coupled with the strength of *Bamanaya* among these people, helped keep this tradition alive.

Once the key is made, the blacksmith can proceed to create the remainder of the locking device. The teeth of the key are placed in embers until they are red hot. The key is then inserted into the canal that is on the posterior side of the horizontal beam, and the teeth pressed up against the underside of its superior border. The teeth char the points of contact through which the blacksmith then punctures holes. These holes must be of sufficient diameter to both accommodate the teeth and the pins.

Illus. 61a.
The two suspended locking pins of the lock depicted in Illus. 29 and Figure 16 in the Catalogue section (Photograph by Marli Shamir).

With the horizontal beam pushed to the left in the locked position, the blacksmith again heats the teeth in embers until they are red hot, and then inserts the key into the canal. He presses the teeth up into the holes previously made in the superior border of the beam, and these make contact with the roof of the cavity in the vertical beam. He then sculpts out a small recess in the vertical beam above the cavity, and punctures holes in its floor through which the pins can fall. The heated pins are inserted through these holes, and their tops bent to prevent them from completely falling through. The

Illus. 61b.
The metal key inserted into a superior opening of the horizontal beam. Its two teeth fit into the corresponding two holes in the superior border of the horizontal beam (Photograph by Marli Shamir).

recess is sculpted with sufficient height so that the pins can completely retract upward when the lock is opened.

The blacksmith must be sure that the teeth of the key precisely match the holes in the superior border of the horizontal beam and disengage the pins. The lock is in effect opened by putting the key into the back of the horizontal beam and engaging its teeth into the holes filled with the dangling pins. Once this is done, the teeth are pushed up, disengaging the pins, and the horizontal beam pulled to the right, thus removing it from its hole in the door frame.

Some blacksmiths place a metal strip over the superior border of the horizontal beam between the two lips in order to protect it from wear; that is the surface subjected to the most friction as the horizontal beam is pulled outward and upward on opening the lock.[42]

Illus. 61c.
With the horizontal beam in the locked position, the pins are engaged in the two holes on its superior border. The metal key is shown inserted into the canal (Photograph by Marli Shamir).

Once the mechanical components of a lock are completed, the blacksmith refines the surfaces of both beams and prepares them for pyroengraved or gouged-out signs. Not all locks bear these signs, and sometimes only the vertical beam does. The placement of these signs is called *lafyen tiw*, which literally means "the pause of the signs." Pyroengraving is achieved with the red-hot blade of a sharp knife (*mourou*). The choice of graphic signs is frequently but not necessarily determined by the overall symbolism of the lock. At the time of pyroengraving, holes are bored into the top and bottom of the vertical beam to accommodate the flat, triangular-headed nails used to affix locks to doors.

Illus. 61d. The two teeth of the metal key are pushed up into the two holes in the superior border of the horizontal beam, disengaging the pins (Photograph by Marli Shamir).

The final stage in the creation of a lock involves charring certain parts of it through the use of red-hot blades (*sonbèw*) of varying widths applied to the wood. Although locks in Western collections often appear to have a uniform color, at the time of their creation certain surfaces are left in their natural wood state (Figure 15 in the Catalogue section). Usually the head and legs (if any) are charred along with the lateral sides of the vertical beam and the superior and inferior surfaces of the horizontal beam.[43] Once locks are affixed to doors, women apply shea butter (*Vitellaria paradoxa*) and kitchen soot to them. Locks also acquire patina through use and the accretion of dirt and food residues.

Illus. 61e. With the pins disengaged, the horizontal beam is pulled and the tapered end of the lock slides out of its hole in the doorway masonry (Photograph by Marli Shamir).

Bamana Terms for the Parts of Locks

The Bamana use specific terms for the various parts of locks that provide insight into their general overall symbolic meaning. The vertical beam is called mother (*ba*), while the horizontal one is known as father (*fa*). The posterior cavity in the vertical beam in which the bolt slides is called *naga* (lower abdomen). The superior border of this cavity through which the locking pins pass is called *soroyoro* (find, place). This is a euphemism for vagina used by men to indicate possession of a woman for the purpose of coital pleasure. [44] The superior edge of the horizontal beam (bolt) is called *den* (child). [45]

The locking pins are known as *gni* (teeth), while the key is called *konègè* (door, iron). The teeth on the end of the key are called *konègègni* (door, iron, teeth). [46] When the teeth of the key are engaged in the holes of the horizontal beam and in contact with the locking pins, they are known as *fa kili* (father, egg), while the latter are called *ba kili* (mother, egg). This terminology refers to the eggs many Bamana believe women have in their lower abdomens, and to a man's semen. Thus, the insertion of the key symbolizes insemination and impregnation.[47] The key also symbolizes the relationship between husband and wife.[48]

A half century ago, Paques, working among the Samaké group of Bamana in the Cercle of Bougouni, documented that the vertical beam represented the wife, the horizontal one the husband, and the fixation of the lock by nails, consummation of the marriage. According to Paques, the wife ordered the vertical beam from the blacksmith while the husband did the same for the horizontal one. [49] As Tesi notes, the shape of the horizontal beam, and especially its tapered end, resembles a penis.[50] Similarly, the sliding action of the horizontal beam evokes the physical act of sexual intercourse. Blacksmiths with whom I studied were very clear about the fact that the vertical beam represents a woman, the horizontal one a man, and that together they symbolize marriage and guarantee fertility.[51]

Variations in Lock Placement

The usual placement of a lock is on the left side of a door. However, rarely they are placed on the right side when the hinge mechanism is on the left. I did observe a lock in the village of Sia in the Arrondissement of Katiena that was originally made for a left-sided door mounting but that had been transferred to another door with left-sided hinges. In order to make this lock functional, the owner reversed the horizontal beam so that its normal posterior surface faced outward. Because the two pins and corresponding holes in the beam were located in the midline, the locking mechanism worked. However, alternative placement of the holes might have resulted in engagement of either one or no pins.

Illus. 62a.
Three-paneled door in the eastern Bamana country with an interior post lock accessed through a hole in the house wall. The wooden key is equipped with two terminal metal pins. Village of Togou, Segou region (Cercle of Segou), 1973.

The Bamana also use locks affixed to posts set in the ground inside a building. This type of mounting is especially common in the eastern Bamana area with doors leading into vestibules. Since this doorway gives access to an extended family's compound, locking it provides security for all the households that are part of it.

A post lock is usually mounted on a post some two feet high, the lower end of which is inserted into the ground, adjacent to the door. Once the insertion is completed, only a small portion of the post remains above ground. The lock is actually mounted on a ledge created by removing two-thirds of the upper anterior face of the post. The remaining posterior third serves as a backing for the lock to which it is affixed with two flat triangular-headed nails. As with locks mounted on doors, the nails are driven through pre-made holes, and both their heads and distal extremities bent to achieve fixation.

Illus. 62b.
The key is inserted through the hole and into the opening on the lateral side of the lock's horizontal beam.

Post locks are often used with left-hinged doors. Access to the lock is provided by a hole in the masonry wall close to the ground. One must insert the key through the hole, which is large enough to accommodate an arm, turn to the left, and place it in the canal of the horizontal beam to disengage the pins. This system has two advantages. The lock is not visible from the outside, and people can lock the door from the inside as well as whenever they leave. However, locks on doors can only be locked from the outside.

Illus. 62c.
The post lock in the locked position with its tapered end blocking the inward opening of the door. The key insertion opening is to the left. Sacrificial material is present on the wall to the left of the door.

The sculpted anterior surface of a post lock usually faces the wall, and often the hollowed-out canal of the horizontal beam does as well to provide ease of access for the key. The fact that the lock faces the outside underscores its primary purpose, which is to provide spiritual protection against sorcery and malevolent *nyama*.

All of the post locks I saw in situ in the eastern Bamana area had horizontal beams providing only lateral access for the key. A superior access with an all-metal key would prove extremely difficult since the opening and closing of post locks is done by hand manipulation only and not by sight. The keys for post locks are wood with metal teeth mounted at right angles at the distal ends.

Symbols and Meanings

The meanings of locks are transmitted through both their overall sculptural form and the graphic signs that are pyroengraved or gouged out on the surfaces of the vertical and horizontal beams. Most locks carry surface graphic signs, but there are exceptions to this rule. In general, the vertical beams are more frequently and more richly pyroengraved than the horizontal ones.

The forms and graphic signs present in locks cannot be literally read in terms of their meanings. Rather, they are symbolic in nature and represent a broad range of philosophical and religious beliefs as well as historic and legendary events and social values that are essential to *Bamanaya*. Complicating matters is the fact that forms are frequently abstract in character, thus rendering them difficult to decipher for those not conversant in the corpus of beliefs and values of *Bamanaya*. As previously mentioned, locks are integrative sculptures that combine form and graphic signs in order to convey underlying beliefs and values, but these meanings are not intended to be understood by everyone. The Bamana rigidly control access to knowledge (and thus to power) based on age, gender, and *dyow* initiation status. Thus, secrecy and ambiguity of meaning often guide spoken language and transmission of symbolic knowledge through sculptural form. To outsiders, it often appears that convoluted deductive reasoning is required to understand Bamana communication, whether as spoken language or as sculpture. Yet the initiated Bamana can easily decipher all these multiple symbols and nuances within familiar logic and belief systems that deny effortless comprehension to the uninitiated. [52]

As previously mentioned, door locks serve as part of an array of measures intended to confront sorcery and manage *nyama*. In this capacity, they are power objects that serve notice to both sorcerers and other malevolent supernatural forces that those who reside behind the doors also have access

to more secret and powerful measures for dealing with them. In addition to this spiritual purpose, door locks have important educative, commemorative, and philosophical purposes for the Bamana. Their functional and utilitarian purposes are only of secondary value, for in reality, it would be an easy matter to break into a house secured by a sculpted lock.

Illus. 63.
Lock depicting the *koro* lizard and demonstrating the insertion of the tapered end of the horizontal beam into the mud masonry of the doorway.
Village of Douale, Banimounitie region (Cercle of Bougouni), 1970.

The forms depicted in locks fall into several categories. Those depicting human beings represent historic or legendary figures, the complementary male-female pair, and social conditions such as orphan status. Many such locks represent *Mouso Koroni Koundyé*, the important female supernatural being who played a crucial role in the creation of life on earth. A number of locks depict animal forms including butterflies, snails, bats, owls, tortoises, lizards, and crocodiles. These forms all carry very specific and important messages for the Bamana, and relate to the creation legends, philosophical and religious beliefs, challenges to Islam, protection from sorcerers, *dyow*, and historical matters. Crocodiles and other lizards are avatars of *Faro*, the powerful deity who provides equilibrium to the world and to men's lives. Thus, their forms as represented in locks are powerful symbols of this deity, and as such provide protection from sorcery and promote fertility, wealth, and happiness.

Illus. 64.
Four-paneled house door and a lock depicting the rudimentary form of the crocodile, a powerful anti-sorcery symbol. Village of Morobougou, Bougouni region (Cercle of Bougouni), 1970.

Illus. 65.
Close-up of upper portion of lock depicted in Illus. 49 and Figure 8 in the Catalogue section. The stylized head represents the power of the *bamada* hat and the open jaws of the crocodile. The upper portion of the anterior surface of the vertical beam is pyroengraved with double-lined lozenges which represent procreative fluids, the four directions of celestial space, cosmic waters, and procreation. Djitoumou region (Cercle of Bamako) (Photograph by Marli Shamir).

A large number of locks represent the *Komo* society by incorporating its knowledge and power symbols in abstract form. These include a prominent neck, crocodile jaws, and the stylized form of the *bamada* hat worn by the leaders of this *dyow*. The power of the *Komo* is also projected in a lock form representing a bard (*dyeli*) who challenged its power by attending one of its ceremonies without permission. The bard was later poisoned by *korté* and died. The lock commemorating this legendary event clearly communicates the power of the *Komo* and how its powers prevailed over those of Islam (Figure 27 in the Catalogue section). The Islam-*Bamanaya* conflict is also depicted in a lock representing a smoking pipe (*taba da*). This clear symbolic challenge to Islam is popularly recounted in a legendary story well known among the Bamana (Figure 39 in the Catlogue section.)

A number of historic personages are also depicted in locks, though many of them are only locally known. This renders it difficult to interpret such locks once they are removed from their village contexts. Such locks, as well as others, provide a point of departure for an educative effort to familiarize people with historical events, social conflicts, and serious injustices. This educative purpose of locks does not lessen their other role as power objects to manage *nyama* and thwart sorcery. [53]

It follows that the forms of locks communicate complex messages. These messages are often integrated with those of the graphic signs incised on the vertical and horizontal beams. These signs (*nèguè misen* or *tiw*) are also complex in their meanings. They are power symbols that not only convey social, philosophical, and religious messages, but which also enhance a lock's ability to achieve its protective and educative purposes. [54]

During the course of my original field research, some younger informants told me that locks represented family or village totems (*tanaw*), but senior sculptor-blacksmiths disputed this interpretation. [55] Since that time, additional research has revealed that this interpretation of symbolic meaning probably arose among younger people who had not had a close association with *Bamanaya*, and many of its essential beliefs and values. Being Moslems, they gave these sculptures a newer meaning that is an accepted part of the Islamic lexicon. [56] As totemic representations, locks are more easily retained by those who have drifted away from *Bamanaya* and closer to Islam. In using this form of adaptation, some Bamana are able to preserve an important link to ancestral *nyama* while making locks an acceptable part of the newer religious context in which they find themselves. [57]

Illus. 66.
The stylized upper portion of the lock depicted in Figure 7 in the Catalogue section. It is endowed with the *Komo* symbols of a prominent neck, crocodile jaws, and the *bamada* hat. The anterior surface of the *bamada* hat is pyroengraved with lozenges as is the anterior surface of the upper part of the vertical beam. The lozenges symbolize procreative fluids, the four directions of celestial space, cosmic waters, and procreation.
A triple-lined X is immediately below, its lateral sides filled in with lozenges. This X represents fertility, the universe, man, the four cardinal angles, and *Pemba's* cosmic travels. Djitoumou region (Cercle of Bamako)
(Photograph by Marli Shamir).

Attaching Locks To Doors

The attachment of locks to doors is a task usually accomplished by a blacksmith. In recent decades, this was done without the performance of any ceremonies or celebrations. However, in the distant past, this attachment was cause for a family celebration. A larger communal celebration occurred when the lock depicted a social victim such as an orphan, an unhappy wife, or a slave. The creation of such locks had broad educative social goals. Therefore, their first public display was an important event accompanied by the singing of specific songs whose words recounted the injustice through the tale of a legendary victim.

This practice was no longer extant in the areas where I studied locks in the late 1960s and 1970s. However, a number of my informants recalled the practice as having disappeared well before World War II. Siriman Fané of Koké in the Segou area, who was probably born around 1900, said, "They did this when I was a child." Balou Traoré of Sirakoro in Djitoumou, which is in the western Bamana area, was born around 1890. At the outset of World War I, he was recruited into the Tirailleurs Sénégalais and fought at the battle of the Somme. He said of the practice, "This was done when I was very young. It was not done when I returned from the war." These accounts seem to support the conclusion that this practice had disappeared in many areas in the early part of the twentieth century.

Tesi documented this practice in Bougouni, and also reported that specific phrases of a song's text were connected to corresponding surface areas of the pyroengraved vertical beam. [58] This custom must have been extinct for a very long time in the Kéléya area, as blacksmiths there at the time of Tesi's research in 1971 had not sculpted locks for many years.[59]

Expressing the Essence of *Bamanaya*

Locks are the most public of Bamana sculpture. Unlike other objects which are only periodically displayed or never at all, they are constantly visible to everyone, including children. They not only educate and protect, but also link present generations to their distant ancestors. They are simultaneously religious icons, utilitarian objects, and works of art. Their mechanical strength matters less than their magical powers, and their social commentaries are communicated through symbols rather than words. Locks extol marriage, promote fertility, symbolize the gods, and direct social conduct. The lessons they teach speak of the creation of the universe, the value of balance, order and harmony, and the need for stability and equilibrium in the world. They encourage virtue, condemn disorder, praise heroic ancestors, and disparage villains.

Locks attached to doors in Bamana villages express the essence of *Bamanaya*. When transported to the pages of a published volume or when exhibited in museum cases, their original spiritual voices may be stilled. They may no longer speak of the gods and ancestors, nor of the rightness of things in the conduct of human affairs. Rather, they can be heard to speak in a different language that uses only the lexicon of art. Yet, their original spiritual voices are still there, ready to speak to those who are willing to listen.

REFERENCES

1.	For a superb detailed analysis of the traditional architecture and layout of Bamana villages, see Brasseur, Gérard. *Les Etablissements humains au Mali.* Dakar: IFAN, 1968, 261–320. This volume also contains excellent descriptions of the buildings, shelters, and settlement and village plans of other ethnic groups in Mali. In the average Bamana village of five hundred people, there may be only fifteen or so *gouaw*.

2.	For a detailed pictorial overview of West African portals and doorways, see Barry, Rahim Danto. *Portes d'Afrique.* Paris: Norma Editions, 1999.

3.	The word *dankoun* derives from *da* (portal, doorway, mouth) and *koun* (head, top of, beginning of). See Bazin, Mgr. H. *Dictionnaire Bambara-Français.* Paris: Imprimerie Nationale, 1906, 94, 333–334.

4.	The term *folo maou dou da* derives from *folo* (formerly, of old, of yore), *maou* (people), *dou* (compound), and *da* (portal, doorway, mouth). *Galé* means times past, or antiquity. See Bazin. *Dictionnaire,* 94–95, 207, 223. For an excellent depiction and discussion of ancestral portals, see Colleyn, Jean Paul and De Clippel, Catherine. *Bamanaya. Un'arte di vivere in Mali/Un art de vivre au Mali.* Milan: Centro Studi Archeologia Africana, 1998, 42–46.

5.	Personal observations made in the field in Mali during the 1960s and 1970s. In the village of Zambougou, Arrondissement of Markala, Cercle of Segou, people asked that I not photograph these sacrifices.

6.	*Binakoun* is derived from *bi* (to fall, to lower) and *koun* (head, top of, beginning of). Another term for threshold is *bondakoun* which is derived from *bonda* (exit, way out) and *koun*. See Bazin. *Dictionnaire,* 83–84, 333–334.

7.	Interviews with Moussa Coulibaly, master sculptor–blacksmith, Touganabougou, Arrondissement of Markala, Cercle of Segou, Mali, 1970–1971. Interviews with Makan Fané, master sculptor-blacksmith, Arrondissement of Niossombougou, Cercle of Kolokani, Mali, 1967–1974. This and related practices were still being observed in some villages in the 1990s (Personal communication, Amadou Sanogo, Segou, Mali, March 15, 1999).

8.	Paques, Viviana. Les Samake. *Bulletin de l'IFAN* 1956, Series B, 3–4, 369–385.

9.	For an important discussion of *dibi*, see McNaughton, Patrick. *Secret Sculptures of Komo. Art and Power in Bamana (Bambara) Initiation Societies.* Philadelphia, PA: Institute for the Study of Human Issues, 1979, 44. In a practical sense, the bush was an especially dangerous place for the Bamana at night when predators such as lions, hyenas, and leopards were present in significant numbers. However, these species declined to residuary numbers during the first decades of the twentieth century. It is tempting to theorize that the Bamana association of night and darkness with danger evolved in part during a time when certain nocturnal species posed a real physical threat.

10.	Personal observations made in the field in Mali during the 1960s and 1970s. In the village of Ngobola in the Cercle of Segou, I observed regular sacrifices on the exterior walls of doorways during the early 1970s. Blood and millet porridge sacrifices were also made over the thresholds of vestibules to invoke the protection of ancestral spirits. The people of this village were known throughout the area at the time as being strong adherents to *Bamanaya*. To prove the power of the village's *boliw*, the chief boasted to me that iron had never penetrated his skin, and that it never would. This was in response to my request that he be vaccinated against yellow fever through the scarification method that uses a metal stylet.

11.	In the mid-twentieth century, Paques recorded that some Bamana (the Samaké) in the Cercle of Bougouni smeared fresh cow dung around the perimeters of their doorways every fifteen days. They also made regular sacrifices to their ancestors on house walls. These sacrifices, as in other areas of the Bamana country, consist of millet porridge mixed with chicken blood and feathers. At the time, these Bamana also periodically spread a mixture of cow dung and the ashes of the bark of *da guo* (*Hibiscus exculentus*) on the floors of their houses in order to keep out malevolent forces. See Paques. Les Samaké, 388.

12.	For a fuller discussion of the symbolism of doors and their relationship to silence, secrecy, and tranquility, see Zahan, Dominique. *La Dialectique du verb chez les Bambara.* Paris: Mouton & Co., 1963, 9–10, 155.

13.	Adzes are known as *sèmèw* (singular *sèmè*) or *dèsèlanw* (singular *dèsèlan*). For a fuller description of Bamana sculpting tools and techniques, see McNaughton, Patrick R. *The Mande Blacksmith. Knowledge, Power, and Art in West Africa.* Bloomington and Indianapolis: Indiana University Press, 1988, 22–39; and Brett-Smith, Sarah C. *The Making of Bamana Sculpture. Creativity and Gender.* Cambridge: Cambridge University Press, 1994, 137–202.

14.	In 1967, this writer had two house doors and frames made in Timbuctoo. They were made by Alhaje Boucar

Maiga, *maître menuisier* (master carpenter), from wood brought up from the Ivory Coast by truck and boat. Maiga's workshop produced many of the doors used on buildings in Timbuctoo at that time. One of the doors was made for the late Dr. George I. Lythcott, and the other for myself. The latter was placed on exhibition in 1974 at the Martin and Osa Johnson Safari Museum in Chanute, Kansas, and donated to the museum in 1985. It is now part of the permanent exhibition of African art in the museum's Imperato African Hall. For a photograph of this door and details about it, see Robbins, Warren M. and Nooter, Nancy Ingraham. *African Art in American Collections*. Washington DC, and London: Smithsonian Institution Press, 1989, 535. See also Songhoi, House Door and Frame. In Imperato, Pascal James. *The Cultural Heritage of Africa*. Chanute, Kansas: Safari Museum Press, 1974, 5–6.

15. Interviews with the late Modjie Samaké, village of Senou, Arrondissement Central, Cercle of Bamako, Mali, 1969–1971. Additional information was provided by Modjie Samaké's grandsons, Aliou Coulibaly and his half-brother, Amadou Coulibaly, during the period 1967–2000. Modjie Samaké died in 1972 at the age of ninety-four. The time line for her life events was established by her recollections of other occurrences such as the occupation of nearby Bamako by the French in 1883, and their conquest of Segou in 1890. Understandably, the dates provided for Modjie Samaké's birth and marriage represent estimates.

16. In April 1970, I was traveling in the eastern part of the Cercle of Kita, and encountered a young woman and her entourage standing on the outskirts of the village of Djigila. She was being married to an older man who already had a senior wife. She and her friends and relatives were carrying all of her household goods as well as a newly made door which lacked a lock. The door had been given to her by her parents, and was affixed that day to the doorway of her new home.

17. The ceremony of stone placement is known as *senk-outourou* (foot, stretch). See Tesi, Paule. *Introduction à l'étude des serrures Bambara. Memoire de maîtrise*. Paris, 1972, 13 (microfiche). For detailed descriptions of Bamana marriage customs, see Paques, Viviana. *Les Bambara*. Paris: Presses Universitaires de France, 1954, 93–94; and Zahan. *La Dialectique*, 85–95.

18. Although the majority of doors are hinged on the right, there are some whose hinges are sculpted on the left. This is especially true in the eastern Bamana area where post locks are used for securing doors. For the Bamana, the right symbolizes male and the left female.

19. In 1967, while investigating a severe epidemic of measles, I observed a sculpted Bamana granary door in the village of Boala, Cercle of Kokokani. It depicted a lizard (crocodile) on the right–sided panel. Local missionaries at the Faladie Catholic Mission informed me that they had seen a few similar sculpted doors in other nearby villages, but that overall they were rare. Because of the recent high mortality from measles among the children of Boala, the village elders suspected that the epidemic was due to sorcery. They were especially sensitive about photographs being taken of any doors in the village, explaining that such an action might reduce their protective powers by removing some of their *nyama*. Large sculpted vestibule doors were still present in situ in the 1960s among the Somono and Bozo, two groups of Niger River fishermen with cultural ties to the Bamana. For a fuller description of these two groups, see N'Diayé, Bokar. *Groupes ethniques au Mali*. Bamako: Editions Populaires, 1970, 418–441; and Ligers, Z. *Les Sorko (Bozo). Maîtres du Niger. Etude ethnographique*. Paris: Librairie des cinq continents, 1964 (Volume I), 1966 (Volume II), 1967 (Volume III), 1969 (Volume IV). For additional comments about these doors, see Tesi. *Introduction*, 11.

20. See Rodriques, Georges D. *A Collection of West African Doors and Locks*. New York: Arte Primitivo Inc., 1968, 8; and Duthoy, Pascal. Gesculpteerde deursloten bij de Bamana en de Dogon. *Vereniging Vrienden Van Ethnografica* 1999, 66:46–51. For a detailed structural analysis of Dogon, Bamana, and Senufo doors and locks, see Suys, Bart. *Sculptural versierde deuren en deursloten bij de Dogon, de Bambara, en de Senufo (West Afrika)*. Licenciate thesis. Ghent: Rijksuniversiteit Gent, 1983. For an early exhibition of locks, see Imperato, Pascal James. West African Door Locks. Tribal Arts Gallery Two, New York, June 1974. *African Arts* 1974, VIII(1):68.

21. Personal observations made in the field in Mali during the 1960s and 1970s.

22. For details on the men who were recruited into the French armed forces from the western Bamana area, see Balesi, Charles John. *From Adversaries to Comrades-in-Arms: West Africans and the French Military, 1885–1918*. Waltham: Crossroads Press, 1979; and Echenberg, Myron. *Colonial Conscripts. The Tirailleurs Sénégalais in French West Africa, 1957–1960*. London: J. Currey, 1991. See also Tesi. *Introduction*, 2.

23. See Kaba, Lansiné. *The Wahhabiyaya. Islamic Reform and Politics in French West Africa*. Evanston, IL: Northwestern University Press, 1974.

24. Tesi. *Introduction*, 3.

25. During the 1940s and 1950s, Sidiki Sanogo was a leading Marka Moslem cleric in the Arrondissement of Markala, Cercle of Segou. He enjoyed a very high status among Moslems because of his ability to destroy with impunity masks, *boliw*, and other material expressions of *Bamanaya*. Village elders often called on him to rid them of these objects

once they had "begun to pray." He would frequently throw the objects into large holes in baobob trees or burn them. Of interest is the fact that he kept a post lock (Figure 43 in the Catalogue section) to secure the door of his own vestibule long after he had begun destroying sculpture for other villages. Neither he nor his son (Mahamoutou) and grandson (Amadou) saw any inherent contradiction in his and their continued use of this lock and his destruction of sculpture in other villages. This was due to the fact that he had commissioned the lock during the 1930s within an Islamic cultural context. The lock was sculpted in the form of an iguana which was then a widely accepted form among certain Moslems in this region and elsewhere. Neither he nor his descendants considered the lock as having its origins in *Bamanaya*. Rather, they viewed it as a reflection of Islamic belief. For Sanogo was an adherent of the *Tidjaniya Sufi* order that had been popularized in this area of Mali in the mid–nineteenth century by the Tukulor Moslem warrior, El Hadj Omar Tall. A popular legend among this group holds that Tall brought back a sacred iguana from his pilgrimage to Mecca and released it in the town of Nioro which he had conquered in 1854. They believe that the descendants of this iguana are capable of verifying the purity of Moslems who come to a mosque to pray and hit the impure with their tails. See Imperato, Pascal James. *A Wind in Africa. A Story of Modern Medicine in Mali.* St. Louis: Warren H. Green, Inc., 1975, 281. The importance of iguanas to the *Tidjaniya* no doubt accounts in part for the popularity of this form in locks once sculpted in the eastern Bamana country (Interviews with the late Mahamoutou Sanogo, Boussin, Arrondissement of Markala, Cercle of Segou, Mali, 1968–1974, and with Amadou Sanogo, Boussin, Segou, and Bamako, Mali, 1968–2000).

26.   In 1973, I was visiting Siriman Fané, then an elderly master sculptor–blacksmith in the Arrondissement of Markala. He was one of my research informants, and a leading sculptor of marionettes. While sitting in his forge, I noticed a pile of old marionettes in a far corner. Siriman said that the *ton* of the village of Koké had ordered new ones to improve the quality and competitiveness of their performances, and had discarded those which he had sculpted in the 1950s. He had made new marionettes for the *ton* over the preceding year. Siriman offered to sell me the ten marionettes for a very nominal amount. They were brightly painted with modern oil paints, and were thus not highly sought after by African art collectors. He assured me that their *nyama* would do me no harm. In 1997, I donated these marionettes as well as a pair of *Tyi Wara* sculptured by Siriman to the Smithsonian Institution's National Museum of Natural History. The latter sculptures were placed on permanent exhibition in 1999 in the museum's new permanent exhibition, *African Voices.* At the same time, I also donated Siriman's large *yayoroba* puppet which he had sculpted in 1970, and a pair of *Tyi Wara*, and a statue sculpted by his nephew, Bafing Kané. For details on the *yayoroba* perfor-

mance, see Imperato, Pascal James. The *Yayoroba* Puppet Tradition of Mali. *The Puppetry Journal* 1981, 32(4):20–26; and Imperato, Pascal James. The Depiction of Beautiful Women in Malian Youth Association Masquerades. *African Arts* 1994, XXVII(1):58–65, 95. In 1970, I acquired a lock from Siriman that he had sculpted in the 1930s for a family in the nearby village of Miniankabougou. They had converted to Islam, and after removing it returned it to him (See Figure 44 in the Catalogue section).

27.   See Note 25 for a fuller explanation of the symbolism of the iguana for the *Tidjani* Tukulor.

28.   There may obviously be other explanations for the lack of form diversity I observed in Segovian locks in situ in the latter part of the twentieth century. However, many Bamana informants said that the Tukulor forced their ancestors to remove door locks, and permitted only those depicting the iguana (Interviews with Karamako Kanté, sculptor–blacksmith, Ngoloba, Arrondissement of Markala, Cercle of Segou, Mali, 1968–1974; and Siriman Fané, Koké, Arrondissement of Markala, Cercle of Segou, Mali, 1970–1974). It is noteworthy that while other materials and cultural expressions of Bamanaya survived the almost thirty years of Tukulor rule, the tradition of sculpting a diversity of lock forms did not. This raises the question of whether great diversity of form really existed immediately before Tukulor rule as claimed by Bamana traditionalists in the late twentieth century.

29.   Tauxier, Louis. *La Religion Bambara.* Paris: Librairie Paul Geuthner, 1927, 300–301.

30.   During my field research in the 1960s and 1970s, I encountered many young blacksmiths who had never sculpted a lock, and older ones who had not done so in many years. Tesi made similar observations in 1971. See Tesi. *Introduction*, 3.

31.   Diallo, Yaya and Hall, Mitchell. *The Healing Drum: African Wisdom Teachings.* Rochester, Vermont: Destiny Books, 1989, 191–192. The Mininaka live to the southeast of the Bamana and are linguistically related to the Senufo. As such, they are considered to be a Voltaic people and not Mande as are the Bamana. Although some of their practices and beliefs are similar to those of the Bamana, and may perhaps have been adopted from the latter, the Bamama consider them to be a distinct and separate people. For a fuller discussion of the Minianka and their beliefs and practices see Jonckers, Danielle. *La Société Miniyanka du Mali. Traditions communautaires et développement cotonnier.* Paris: Editions L'Harmattan, 1987; Colleyn, Jean-Paul. *Les Chemins de Nya. Culte de possession au Mali.* Paris: Editions de l'Ecole des Hautes Etudes en Science Sociales, 1988; and Jespers, Philippe. Mask and Utterances: The Analysis of an "Auditory" Mask in the Iniatory Society of the Komo Minyanka, Mali. In *Objects: Signs of Africa.* Edited by Luc de Heusch. Ghent : Snoeck-Ducaju & Zoon, 1996, 37–56.

51

32.   Tesi interprets *bara bara* as meaning "large gourd." This interpretation is perfectly correct. See Tesi. *Introduction*, 9. However, the meaning "protuberance" seems much more specific to door locks. Several of my informants interpreted the term in this manner when applied to locks, and not as meaning a "large gourd." The components of the term *kon-barabara* can be written separately as *kon bara bara*. See Tesi. *Introduction*, 9. However, most standard dictionaries write it as one term. See Bazin. *Dictionnaire*, 308–309; and Molin, Msgr. *Dictionnaire Bambara-Français et Français-Bambara*. Issy-les-Moulineaux: Les Presses Missionaires, 1955, 355. Because of significant regional variations in the pronunciation of *Bamana-kan*, *konbarabara* can often sound like *konbala-bala* when used to designate door locks. See Imperato, Pascal James. Door Locks of the Bamana of Mali. *African Arts* 1972, 5(3):52–56, 84.

33.   A number of authors have commented on the ancient origins of the locking device used in Bamana locks. See Guariglia, G. *L'Arte dell'Africa Nera e il Suo Messagio*. Parma: Edizione Ismes, 1966; von Luschan, Felix. Uber Schlösser mit Fullriegeln. *Zeitschrift für Ethnologie* 1916, 48: 406–429; Paques. Les Samaké, 388; and Pitt-Rivers, Augustus Henry Lane-Fox. *On the Development and Distribution of Primitive Locks and Keys*. London: Chatto and Windus, 1883.

34.   For details concerning Dogon locks, see Calame-Griaule, Geneviève, Dupuis, Annie, and Ndiaye, Francine. *Serrures Dogon. Approche ethnomorphologique*. Paris: Département d'Afrique Noire, Laboratoire d'Ethnologie, Musée de l'Homme, 1976 (microfiche); Dieterlen, Germaine. La Serrure et sa clef (Dogon, Mali). In *Echanges et Communications. Mélanges Offert à Claude Levi-Straus*, edited by J. Poullon and P. Marasse. Paris, The Hague: Mouton, 1970, Volume 1, 7–27; and Imperato, Pascal James. Dogon Door Locks. *African Arts* 1978, XI(4):54–57, 96.

35.   Imperato. Door, 55–56.

36.   Calame-Griaule et al. *Serrures*, 91.

37.   The descriptions concerning the sculpting of locks are given here in the present tense. However, the paucity of locks being sculpted in the early twenty-first century renders these descriptions largely historical in many areas.

38.   For details on these woods, see Berhaut, Jean. *Flore du Sénégal*. Second Edition. Dakar: Editions Clairafrique, 1967, 16, 62, 228, 230, 244. See also Tesi. *Introduction*, 24. Tesi found a clear distinction in wood use for doors and locks in the Bougouni area. However, I did not find such distinctions in the northern and eastern Bamana areas, perhaps due to limited tree choice as a result of progressive environmental degradation.

39.   For details concerning these rituals, see Brett-Smith. *The Making*, 131–137.

40.   The *Tyi Wara* headdresses sculpted by Bafing Kané were donated by this writer to the Smithsonian Institution's National Museum of Natural History in 1997, along with other objects sculpted by him and his uncle, Siriman Fané.

41.   For a description of Bamana sculpting tools, see McNaughton. *The Mande*, 22–39; and Tesi. *Introduction*, 25.

42.   The information presented here on the sculpting of locks and the manufacturing of their locking devices was pro-vided by several blacksmiths including Moussa Coulibaly (Touganabougou), Makan Fané (Bamako and Niosombougou), Siriman Fané (Koké), Bafing Kané (Koké), and Karamako Kanté (Ngoloba). For details on working iron and sculpting wood, see Brett-Smith. *The Making*, 119–202; and McNaughton. *The Mande*, 22–37. While doing field research in the western Bamana area in the Arrondissement of Kéléya in 1971, Tesi observed a similar process for making locks. See Tesi. *Introduction*, 23–27. The Bamana use several terms to connote locking a door. These include *kon sogo* (door, lock with a key), and *soda souara* (one has closed the room with a key). These terms can be used with traditionally sculpted locks as well as with modern locks of various kinds.

43.   For new locks photographed in the field in Mali, see McNaughton. *The Mande*, Plate I.

44.   See Bazin. *Dictionnaire*, 556, 686; and Tesi. *Introduction*, 15.

45.   Interviews with Kolékélé Mariko and Amadou Sanogo, Bamako, Mali, 1996.

46.   There are a number of variants for these terms. These include: *kounyè* (head, iron), *konnègè* (door, iron), *konègènyi* (door, iron, teeth), *nyi* (teeth), *nin* (teeth), and *gnin* (teeth).

47.   Many Bamana are aware of the association between eggs and semen in procreation from their observations of birds, especially domestic poultry. However, some believe that women become pregnant through a man's heavy breath entering their nostrils during intercourse (Interviews in the Arrondissements of Dioro, Katiena, and Markala, Cercle of Segou, 1968–1974).

48.   Based on information provided by the noted Malian anthropologist, Youssouf Cissé, Tesi relates that the key teeth were traditionally two in number, and that they represent the bifurcated penile glans of the lizard *Agama agama*, known in *Bamanan-kan* as *basa*. See Tesi. *Introduction*, 15.

49.   Paques. *Les Samaké*, 388. I was not able to corroborate this practice in other Bamana areas.

50.   See Tesi. *Introduction*, 15.

51.   Interviews with Moussa Coulibaly (Touganabougou), Makan Fané (Bamako and Niosombougou), Siriman Fané (Koké), Bafing Kané (Koké), and Karamoko Kanté, (Ngoloba).

52.   As pointed out elsewhere, the Bamana value silence and its use as a modulator of speech. They also believe that speech must be carefully controlled, and that great harm can result if it is not. Locks are intimately connected to knowledge and communication, and hence to speech. One of the ways the Bamana try to silence the bitter words of an enemy is to prepare a paste-like concoction from the bark of seven caicedrat trees (*Khaya sénégalensis*) known in *Bamanan-kan* as *dala*. The resulting bitter paste is then secretly inserted into the holes of the horizontal beam of the enemy's lock; thus the lock is silenced because it can no longer function. The bitter bark used in this concoction also reflects the bitterness caused by the enemy's speech. Once the lock is blocked and rendered mute and powerless, the enemy is also silenced. See Zahan. *La Dialectique*, 158, 160–161, 163–164; and Fraser, Douglas. *African Art as Philosophy*. New York: Interbook, 1974, 85.

53.   Tesi documented similar categories of locks in the Bougouni area. See Tesi. *Introduction*, 2, 19–22.

54.   The fifty-nine Bamana locks presented in the Catalogue section of this volume, including four attached to doors, represent a comprehensive spectrum of the forms created by blacksmiths in past decades. Each lock is accompanied by a lengthy caption that presents detailed information and interpretations of form and graphic sign meaning within the context of *Bamanaya*. I believe that this approach will prove more useful to readers than coverage of this material in this section of the volume.

55.   Moussa Coulibaly (Touganabougou), Makan Fané (Niosombougou), Siriman Fané (Koké), Bafing Kané (Koké), all senior sculptor-blacksmiths, dismissed the interpretation of lock forms as representing totems.

56.   For an earlier report on locks being interpreted as representing totems, see Imperato. *Door*, 54. I am grateful to two of my assistants, the late Djigui Diakité and Amadou Sanogo, for clarifying this issue in the field during the 1980s.

57.   One of the earliest and most exhaustive studies of totemism in the western Sudan was carried out by Joseph Brun, a White Fathers missionary, in the early part of the twentieth century. He clearly states the following in his pioneering work: "Je n'ai jamais rencontré de représentation de l'animal totem, soit sous forme de peinture, sculpture, ou de symbole." ("I have never encountered any representation of a totemic animal, either under the form of a painting, sculpture, or some symbol.") This very definitive statement was made at a time when door locks were widely present in most Bamana and Malinké villages. See Brun, Joseph. *Le Totémisme chez quelques peuples du Soudan Occidental*. *Anthropos* 1910, 5:860.

58.   Tesi's field work was conducted over a three-month period in 1971 in the village of Kéléya in the western Bamana area. Her principal interpreter was Wâ Kamissoko, a highly respected Malinké bard and oral historian from Krina, an area to the west of Kéléya. Many of the field observations reported by Tesi were made by Kamissoko because blacksmiths in the Kéléya area refused to cooperate with her. Given Kamissoko's profession as an oral historian and praise singer, he might have had a clearer orientation toward uncovering the association of song phrases with specific areas of locks. See Tesi. *Introduction*, 4–5. See also Wâ Kamissoko. *L'Empire du Mali: Un récit de Wâ Kamissoko de Krina enregistré, transcrit, traduit et annoté par Yousouf Tata Cissé*. Paris: Fondation SCOA pour la Promotion de la Recherche Scientifique en Afrique Noire, 1975 (Parts I–III), 1978 (Parts IV–V).

59.   Tesi. *Introduction*, 3.

CATALOGUE

CROCODILE JAWS AND THE *KOMO*

Figure 1. H. 15¼ in. (38.7 cm)

This figure represents the *Komo* and its anti-sorcery and educative powers. The two horn-like structures atop the head symbolize the sorcery-destroying powers of the crocodile's jaws. They also portray the index and fifth fingers of the left hand, which when held up are a sign of *Komo* society membership. The prominent neck, a common feature on many locks, represents the *Komo's* knowledge and ability to teach. The flare at the base of the lock symbolizes the tail of the swallow (*nanalékou*). The swallow is *Faro's* aerial messenger who carries his words and symbolizes his power. There are no pyroengraved graphic signs on this lock. The locking device contains two pins, and the key insertion is lateral. Brown patina. Provenance: Cercle of Dioila (Baninko).

Figure 2. H. 15½ in. (39.4 cm)

The *Komo's* ability to destroy sorcery is depicted by the closed crocodile jaws, and its knowledge and power to teach by the prominent neck. The pyro-engraved graphic signs on the vertical beam include diagonal striations and two rows of lozenges. A large double-lined X is centered over the cavity through which the horizontal beam slides. A row of three double-lined Xs near the base repeats this theme. The inferior portion of the vertical beam is stylized into a recessed, anteriorly curving and inverted triangular form representing the head of the python (*mignan*), a symbol of God and a powerful force against sorcery. The horizontal beam does not have any graphic signs. The locking device contains three pins, and the key insertion is superior. Black patina. Provenance: Cercle of Bougouni (Bougouni).

Figure 3. H. 18 in. (45.7 cm)

This large lock carries the power symbols of the *Komo* through its prominent neck and the abstract crocodile jaws arising from its head. The large breasts and penis represent *Faro's* androgynous nature. The two long vertical lines down the forehead speak of *Mouso Koroni Koundyé's* invention of scarification during an early phase of creation. Both the vertical and horizontal beams are engraved with graphic signs. These include rows of single- and double-lined lozenges and a large double-lined X on the horizontal beam. The vertical beam has rows of lozenges and two large double-lined Xs, which are powerful fertility symbols. Three double-lined chevrons are at the base of the vertical beam, representing the early cosmic travels of *Mouso Koroni* and *Faro*. The horizontal beam has rows of lozenges and a large double-lined X. Its superior surface is covered by a protective metal strip. The locking device consists of one pin, and the key insertion is superior. Light brown patina. Provenance: Village of Banagolé, Arrondissement of Dialakoro, Cercle of Kolokani (Bélédougou).

Figure 4. H. 19¼ in. (48.8 cm)

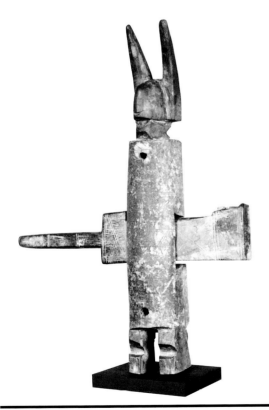

This large and imposing lock depicts a human face without any features except a mouth, which is open. Surrounding the head are the two stylized jaws of the crocodile, symbols of the *Komo's* power to destroy sorcery. The open mouth on the face of this lock reminds people that the mouth is man's great enemy. For through it, man exposes his interior being and unleashes words charged with *nyama* (vital life powers, forces, or energies) whose effects he cannot control. The vertical beam has three graphic signs: diagonal striations, lozenges, and double-lined chevrons. The horizontal beam is dominated by double-lined Xs. The locking device has two pins, and the key insertion is superior. Illustrated in Door Locks of the Bamana of Mali. *African Arts* 1972, V(3), 52–56, 84. Gray patina. Provenance: Cercle of Koulikoro (Bélédougou).

CATALOGUE

Figure 5. H. 14⅛ in. (36.5 cm)

The vertical beam of this lock depicts the power and knowledge of the *Komo*. It also bears two graphic signs: chevrons along the anterior edges, and double-lined Xs in the center. The horizontal beam has double-lined Xs and lozenges. The locking device has two pins, and the key insertion is lateral. Black patina. Provenance: Cercle of Bougouni (Bougouni).

Figure 6. H. 16¼ in. (41.3 cm)

The *bamada* hat worn by Bamana elders and the *Komo tigui* (leader of the *Komo*) is depicted in a highly stylized fashion in this lock as an elliptical structure behind the head. As in most locks symbolizing the *Komo*'s powers, the face lacks a mouth. The vertical beam is pyroengraved with circles, lozenges, and a large, double-lined X above the cavity through which the horizontal beam slides. The recessed, anteriorly curving, and inverted triangular shape at the base of the vertical beam represents the head of the python (*mignan*), a symbol of God. The horizontal beam has several double-lined chevrons across its surface. The locking device has two pins, and the key insertion is superior. Black patina. Provenance: Cercle of Kolondieba (Bougouni).

Figure 7. H. 18¼ in. (46.4 cm)

The face of this beautiful lock is highly stylized so that its sides represent the jaws of the crocodile. Behind the face is the *bamada* hat, itself a powerful anti-sorcery symbol that also depicts the wings of the swallow, one of Faro's messengers. Informants in the area from which this lock came said it represented a powerful male ancestor. As such, it is endowed with the *Komo* symbols of a prominent neck, jaws, and *bamada* hat. While its horizontal beam is devoid of pyroengraved graphic signs, its vertical beam has lozenges, chevrons, and three large, triple-lined Xs. The central X lies over the cavity through which the horizontal beam slides, and is framed on its four sides, thus symbolizing the multiplication of species. The anterior surface of the *bamada* hat is pyroengraved with lozenges. The slight left tilt of the head is counterbalanced by what appears to be a similar shift of the large X on the vertical beam. The superior surface of the horizontal beam is covered by a protective metal strip. This lock was probably not affixed to an exterior door, but to a door between rooms because the degree of patina is not accompanied by significant weathering damage. The locking device has two pins, and the key insertion is superior. Illustrated in Door Locks of the Bamana of Mali. *African Arts* 1972; V(3):52–56, 84, and in *African Art in American Collections*. Washington, DC and London: Smithsonian Institution Press, 1989, 536. Brown patina. Provenance: Cercle of Bamako (Djitoumou).

Figure 8. H. 16½ in. (42 cm)

The triangular head of this very finely sculpted lock depicts a stylized *bamada* hat and the open jaws of the crocodile. Said to represent a male ancestor, it clearly carries the symbols of the *Komo*'s anti-sorcery powers as well as its knowledge. A large, pyroengraved, double-lined X lies over that portion of the vertical beam through which the horizontal beam moves. Above and below this are series of double-lined lozenges which also appear on the horizontal beam. The latter is also pyroengraved with a large, double-lined X on its right anterior surface, and is sculpted with an unusual knob on the right side where the key is inserted. This lock was probably used on an interior door between rooms. The locking device has two pins, and the key insertion is superior. Illustrated in Door Locks of the Bamana of Mali. *African Arts* 1972, V(3):52–56, 84, and in *African Art in American Collections*. Washington, DC and London: Smithsonian Institution Press, 1989, 536. Black patina. Provenance: Cercle of Bamako (Djitoumou).

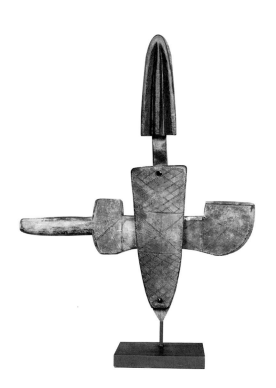

Figure 9. H. 18¼ in. (46.4 cm)

The architectonics of this lock are similar to those in Figure 8. The entire head has been stylized to represent the *bamada* hat, while its anterior surface bears a prominent central nose but no other facial features. The recessed, anteriorly curving, and inverted triangular form at the base of the vertical beam represents the python's head, a symbol of God and a powerful force against sorcery. The vertical beam is incised with rows of double-lined lozenges surrounding a large, central, double-lined X. Four of the latter graphic signs appear on the horizontal beam, whose superior surface is covered by a protective metal sheath. Some informants in the central Bamana area of the Djitoumou claim that this type of lock represents the *kana* (water iguana), an avatar of *Faro* that protects against sorcery and brings good fortune. The locking device contains two pins, and the key insertion is superior. Black patina. Provenance: Cercle of Bamako (Djitoumou).

Figure 10. H. 16¾ in. (42.5 cm)

The *bamada* hat in this lock has been highly stylized into an anteriorly curving open rectangle. While the hat and prominent neck symbolize *Komo* attributes, the central opening in the head represents a *sélé din*, a space into which protective *nyama* can be placed. The head is engraved with double-lined chevrons on the lateral aspects of its sides. The anterior surface of the head has a double-lined X at the top and four sets of scarifications below. At the base of the vertical beam is a recessed, anteriorly curving, and inverted triangular form representing the python's head. The vertical beam bears three sequential double-lined Xs, while the horizontal beam is pyro-engraved with rows of compact, single-lined chevrons throughout. The superior surface of the horizontal beam is covered by metal. The locking device contains three pins, and the key insertion is superior. Gray patina. Provenance: Cercle of Banamba (Bélédougou).

Figure 11. H. 15½ in. (39.4 cm)

The highly stylized *bamada* hat, prominent neck, and absence of a mouth reflect characteristics of the *Komo*. Unlike many locks, the face and forehead bear scarifications. The vertical beam is pyroengraved with a large, central, single-lined X, diagonal striations, and lozenges, while the horizontal beam has double-lined Xs and lozenges. The horizontal beam's superior surface is covered by a protective metal strip. The locking device contains one pin, and the key insertion is superior. Brown patina. Provenance: Cercle of Bamako (Djitoumou).

Figure 12. H. 19¾ in. (50.2 cm)

The head of this remarkable lock has been reduced to the highly stylized form of a square flanked by rectangular ears and is surmounted by an oval representing the *bamada* hat. At the base of the lock is the head of the mythical python (*mignan*), which was created by the light of God. The pyroengraving on the vertical beam has been largely obliterated by successive layers of encrustation, but still reveals some lozenges at the top of the hat. However, the horizontal beam is unusually and richly pyroengraved with double-lined Xs, lozenges, double-lined chevrons, and diagonal striations. The horizontal beam appears to be a replacement, given its prominent pyroengravings and the obliteration of the same on the vertical beam. Its superior surface is covered by a protective metal strip. The locking device contains one pin, and the key insertion is superior. Black patina. Provenance: Cercle of Kolokani (Bélédougou).

CATALOGUE

MOUSO KORONI KOUNDYÉ AND WOMEN

Figure 13. H. 18¼ in. (46.4 cm)

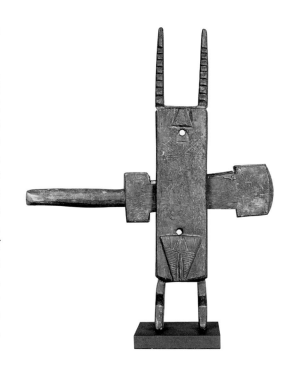

This lock represents *Mouso Koroni Koundyé* (little old woman with a white head), the divine person who played an essential role in the legend of creation. Sculpted in relief at the base of the vertical beam are the realistic elements of the external female genitalia, powerful symbols of fertility and procreation. On either side of the introitus of the vulva are rows of parallel striations representing *Pemba* and his divinity. However, these striations also recall *Pemba's* act of sexual intercourse with *Mouso Koroni* under the form of a block of wood known as the *Pembélé*. They remind viewers that *Mouso Koroni* was physically mutilated during this act, and as a result initiated human circumcision and excision. The triangular shape of a female vulva is repeated in an inverted relief form at the top of the vertical beam, and the latter is surmounted by two parallel serrated forms representing the tails of large black scorpions (*dyonkomiw*). These symbolize *Mouso Koroni's* death from a scorpion sting. The vertical beam is pyroengraved with several rows of lozenges, and also with rows of partial and complete Us, symbols of pregnancy. The horizontal beam is not engraved. Its superior surface is covered by a strip of protective metal. The locking device contains two pins, and the key insertion is superior. Black patina. Provenance: Cercle of Bamako (Djitoumou).

Figure 14. H. 17½ in. (44.5 cm)

Mouso Koroni Koundyé and her sad story are depicted in this lock. The featureless, round head symbolizes her demotion to a nonperson after *Faro* subdued her, and the serrated legs represent scorpion tails. However, the use of scorpion tails for legs on this lock also recalls that blacksmiths attached a dead scorpion to *Mouso Koroni's* leg before burying her. Most of the vertical beam is covered by a large, double-lined X, while at either end is a row of triple-lined chevrons symbolizing *Mouso Koroni's* cosmic travels, and the annual trajectory of the sun. The horizontal beam is not engraved, but the face atop the vertical beam carries a large, double-lined X, partially obscured by encrustation. The horizontal beam's superior surface is covered by a protective metal strip. The locking device contains two pins, and the key insertion is superior. Black patina. Provenance: Cercle of Kita (Birgo).

Figure 15. H. 18¾ in. (47.8 cm)

This lock was sculpted for the author by master blacksmith, Makan Fané in the Bélédougou in April, 1967. Fané intended this lock to represent *Mouso Koroni Koundyé*. He engraved the vertical beam with two double-lined Xs traversed by horizontal lines, representing *Pemba's* introduction of sickness and death. From left to right on the horizontal beam, he first pyroengraved three double-lined Xs, and then two double-lined Xs traversed by vertical lines, the latter having several meanings. These include the six directions of space, and the movement of the universe. This graphic sign also represents the *Komo* and women. Although Fané recognized that several interpretations could be applied to this sign, his intention was for it to represent women. This lock does not contain any holes for affixing it to a door, as Fané knew that the author intended to return with it to the United States. The lack of use permits one to see those portions of a lock initially darkened through surface charring. The locking device contains two pins, and the key insertion is lateral. Brown patina. Provenance: Arrondissement of Niossombougou, Cercle of Kolokani (Bélédougou) (Collection of The Imperato African Gallery, The Martin and Osa Johnson Safari Museum, Chanute, Kansas).

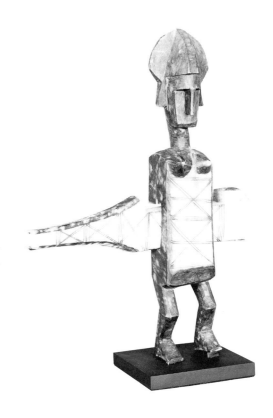

63

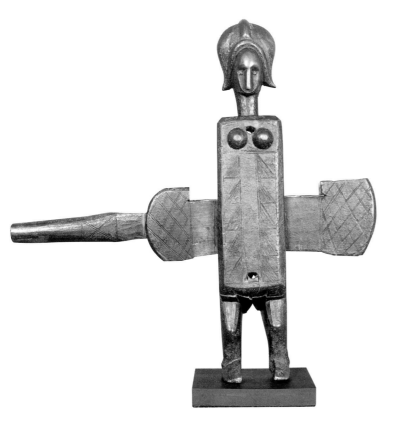

Figure 16. H. 16¼ in. (41.3 cm)

This exceptionally beautiful and richly patinated lock representing *Mouso Koroni Koundyé* was probably affixed to a door between rooms. The delicacy of the overall sculpture is matched by the very fine surface engravings. The edges of the vertical beam are pyroengraved with five successive groups of diagonal striations representing *Pemba* and his association with *Mouso Koroni*. The anterior surface of the horizontal beam has three groups of double-lined lozenges and a double-lined X at the base of the insertion bar. Perfectly aligned with this X is an almost identical one on the posterior surface. Such posterior surface engravings are extremely rare, and this one is unique in this collection of Bamana locks. The superior surface of the horizontal beam is covered by a protective strip of metal. This lock possesses metal eyes which are only occasionally found on these sculptures. Also, buttocks are sculpted on the posterior surface, reflecting the sensibilities of the artist to detail. The locking device contains two pins, and the key insertion is superior. Illustrated in Door Locks of the Bamana of Mali. *African Arts* 1972; V(3):52–56, 84, and in *African Art in American Collections*. Washington, DC and London: Smithsonian Institution Press, 1989, 537. Brown patina. Provenance: Cercle of Bougouni (Bougouni).

CATALOGUE

Figure 17. H. 15⅛ in. (38.4 cm)

The surface designs on the vertical beam of this lock have been largely obliterated by use patina and erosion. The horizontal beam was never pyroengraved with graphic designs. The lock, however, is decorated with a beaded necklace consisting of two coils beneath which are circlets of red thread and white cord. These decorations symbolize *Mouso Koroni Koundyé's* invention of jewelry. The elaborate coiffure, with holes at the base for earrings, symbolizes her invention of hair styling. The locking device consists of one pin, and the key insertion is superior. Brown patina. Provenance: Cercle of Kolokani (Bélédougou).

64

Figure 18. H. 17¾ in. (45 cm)

Several of *Mouso Koroni Koundyé's* acts and characteristics are shown in the great variety of graphic signs displayed on the vertical beam of this lock. In fact, the surface of the vertical beam is one of the most richly engraved of the locks in this collection. The elaborate coiffure symbolizes her invention of hair styling. The forehead is pyroengraved with lozenges, and either side of the face with scarifications. This scarification of the head and face recalls a time at the beginning of creation when humans were unable to speak, and were instructed by *Mouso Koroni* to use facial scarifications as a means of distinguishing women from men. The inferior portion of the vertical beam is stylized into a recessed, anteriorly curving and inverted triangle representing the python's head, a symbol of God, who, as the *Pembélé*, created *Mouso Koroni*. Although the horizontal beam is devoid of graphic signs, the vertical beam is richly pyroengraved. What is unusual about these pyroengravings is not only their diversity, but also their relationships to one another. The top of the vertical beam contains a row of chevrons, some of which are filled in with diagonal striations. Two rows of vertical chevrons are engraved on the left and right edges of the lower half of the beam. While the chevrons alone depict *Mouso Koroni's* cosmic travels and the annual course of the sun, their association with the diagonal striations speaks of *Pemba's* relationship to *Mouso Koroni* and his creation of the sun. Also present on this lock are large circles, two on the anterior surface of the neck, and a horizontal and vertical row below. These circles represent rain, water, *Mouso Koroni's* tears, and fertility. Their association with the chevrons speaks of the rainy season and agricultural fertility. A row of lozenges is also present near the top of the lock, and a large X overlies the cavity through which the horizontal beam passes. Its upper and lower spaces are filled with diagonal striations depicting *Pemba* and his role in fertility and procreation. Striations are present on the sides and posterior surface of the vertical beam. However, these appear to be tool marks rather than graphic signs. The locking device consists of one pin, and the key insertion is superior. Brown patina. Provenance: Cercle of Kolokani (Bélédougou).

Figure 19.   H. 17 in. (44.1 cm)

Although there are few graphic signs on this lock, they clearly speak of *Mouso Koroni Koundyé's* creative acts and her role as the wife of *Pembélé*, the log-like form assumed by *Pemba* during an early phase of creation. The external female genitalia are sculpted in relief at the base of the vertical beam. Immediately above them are a row of diagonal striations representing *Pemba* in his assumed form as *Pembélé*. The juxtapositioning of these two iconographic images symbolizes the act of intercourse between *Pembélé* and *Mouso Koroni*, and the latter's subsequent initiation of circumcision and excision. The pregnant abdomen is engraved with a double-lined X traversed by a horizontal line, reminding people of sickness and death. Two rows of lozenges are below the breasts. The horizontal beam is decorated with chevrons. The locking device consists of two pins, and the key insertion is superior. Brown patina. Provenance: Cercle of Koulikoro (Bélédougou).

Figure 20.   H. 16 in. (40.5 cm)

The elaborate coiffure and the line of circles along the left and right edges of the vertical beam refer to *Mouso Koroni Koundyé* and her creative acts. The vertical beam of this lock is also engraved with two panels of small lozenges surrounding a vertical arrangement of double-lined Xs in the center. The horizontal beam is devoid of graphic signs, but its superior surface is covered by a strip of metal. The locking device consists of two pins, and the key insertion is superior. Black patina. Provenance: Cercle of Bougouni (Bougouni).

Figure 21. H. 16¾ in. (42.5 cm)

Locks such as this one that depict women are common on Bamana doors. Their precise meanings cannot always be inferred from architectonic features and surface designs, for locks with identical features can represent a variety of themes known with precision only to the blacksmiths who sculpted them and to their owners. These locks can represent marital status for women, local female heros, women of special status, ancestors, legendary figures such as Kaba Sira Kamara, who was the wife of a Keita chief, women of unusual accomplishments, and women described in fables and myths. The vertical beam of this lock is supported by legs which are connected to one another to give additional support. It is pyroengraved with two groups of lozenges surrounding a central panel of overlapping double-lined Xs. The horizontal beam does not have any surface engravings. The locking device consists of one pin, and the key insertion is superior. Black patina. Provenance: Cercle of Bamako (Djitoumou).

Figure 22. H. 12½ in. (31.8 cm)

The surfaces of this extremely small lock do not possess any engravings. It is sculpted with a woman's coiffure, and as such could have a variety of meanings. The superior surface of the horizontal beam is covered by a protective strip of metal. The locking device consists of two pins, and the key insertion is superior. Brown patina. Provenance: Cercle of Bamako (Djitoumou).

Figure 23. H. 18 in. (45.8 cm)

This imposing lock depicts a female head that sculpturally projects a sense of great power and strength. Sculpted from a very hard wood, both beams are wider and deeper than the average lock. This greater mass, the powerful head sculpted atop a long, thick neck, and the spear-like configuration of the key insertion end of the horizontal beam infuse this sculpture with what the Bamana would interpret as symbols of great power. The large flare at the base of the vertical beam represents the tail of the swallow (*nanalékou*). This bird symbolizes *Faro* and his powers. Thus, the female figure is supported by the powers of a divine person. The locking device consists of two pins, and the key insertion is lateral. Brown patina. Provenance: Cercle of Bougouni (Bougouni).

COUPLES AND MEN

Figure 24. **Left, H. 19¾ in. (50.1 cm)**

Right, H. 16½ in. (42 cm)

Locks depicting couples are relatively rare. They reinforce the marital theme iconography of locks in general. Both locks shown here appear to have been sculpted by the same hand, and show physical signs of equivalent age and use. The much larger male lock (*left*) and the smaller female one (*right*) have vertical beams whose overall geometric forms approach that of a lozenge. The vertical beam of the male lock has two large, double-lined Xs, and the horizontal beam four. The superior surface of the latter is also covered by a protective metal strip. The figure on the female lock is actually depicted above the vertical beam. Nails have been used to represent both the eyes and earrings. The vertical beam of this lock is engraved with three panels of lozenges which also appear on the torso of the figure. The horizontal beam bears no pyroengravings. The base of the vertical beam is stylized into the head of the python as a recessed, anteriorly curving, and inverted triangular form. The key inserts of the two locks are quite different, the one for the female figure being on the side of the horizontal beam, while that for the male figure is at the top on the right. The key for the female consists of a wooden handle with metal teeth, while that for the male is entirely of metal. Taken individually, these locks could represent many themes. However, their simultaneous use in the same family compound conveys the overriding meaning of marital status and the profound linkages between husband and wife. The unequal social status of men and women is shown dramatically by the difference in the sizes of these locks. In some compounds, the female locks of such couples were affixed to the doors of the *tye so*, a room reserved for the family head and his male friends. The locking device for both locks consists of a pair of pins. Brown patina. Provenance: Cercle of Bamako (Djitoumou).

67

Figure 25. Left, H. 13¼ in. (33.6 cm)

Right, H. 13½ in. (34.4 cm)

The couple representing the marital state is significantly smaller in overall size than the group previously described. The vertical beam of the female figure (*left*) has a row of lozenges at the top and bottom, and down the center. Nails are used to represent eyes. The vertical beam of the male figure (*right*) is covered by three large, interconnected Xs. In a treatment more elaborate than that used on the female lock, the eyes on the male lock originally consisted of metal discs affixed with nails. The horizontal beams contain no surface designs. It is significant that the head of the male lock possesses extremely large, deep ears, symbolizing a husband's ability to keep informed of his wife's words and actions. The key insertion configuration for these locks differs. As with the previous couple, that for the female is on the side while the one for the male is atop the horizontal beam. As on all locks, the sliding of the horizontal beam represents the physical act of intercourse, with the beam itself being viewed as male. The insertion of the key into the end of the horizontal beam of the female lock emphasizes this symbolism. The back of the head of the female lock shows traces of henna (*dyabé*) coloration. The locking device for the female lock consists of two pins while that for the male consists of one. Brown patina. Provenance: Cercle of Koulikoro (Bélédougou).

Figure 26. H. 15½ in. (39.4 cm)

Neither the vertical nor horizontal beams of this lock possesses surface engravings. The head is an almost perfect round sphere, and significantly lacks external ears. The absence of external ears recalls *Faro*, who does not possess them, and the curving legs symbolize the tail of the scorpion that killed *Mouso Koroni Koundyé*. Male locks of this type can have many overall iconographic meanings whose specificity is lost when they are removed from the contexts of their creators and users. They can represent legendary heros, men of special status, notable ancestors, and men described in fables and myths. The locking device consists of two pins, and the key insertion is lateral. Gray patina. Provenance: Cercle of Dioila (Baninko).

Figure 27. H. 14¼ in. (36.2 cm)

This slender lock depicts a male figure with a large open mouth and very prominent ears. These characteristics symbolize bards (*dyéliw*), who are praise singers, oral historians, and social critics. Most bards are excluded from the *Komo* society because of their early conversion to Islam. There is a popular legend among the Bamana and Malinké of an old bard who wanted to be a member of the society, and who eventually told everyone of his plan to attend a *Komo* ceremony. Despite warnings, he witnessed a ceremony of the *Komo*, and shortly thereafter was poisoned by *korté*. The latter is believed by the Bamana to be a small grain of cereal, bone, stone, or wood that can be dispatched through the air by those practicing sorcery. The *korté* enters imperceptibly through the skin, or else finds its way into food or drink. Once poisoned, the body of the old bard began to swell. Realizing that he was dying, he asked the blacksmiths to sculpt a lock in his memory and to affix it to the door of the chief of the bards, telling him that bards should never violate the rules of the *Komo*. The iconography of this lock serves to educate viewers about this tale in three ways. The sign of the *Komo* is an X traversed by a vertical line. This is encoded on the vertical beam from top to bottom by a series of the six upper halves of double-lined Xs traversed by a vertical double line. The central portion of the vertical beam is elevated, representing abdominal swelling, and the five central protuberances on it symbolize the crocodile, an avatar of *Faro*. The right and left sides of the horizontal beam contain several vertical rows of pyro-engraved, crisscrossed signs in which the complete sign of the *Komo* is enmeshed yet clearly visible. While these iconographic messages convey the story of the bard, they also speak of the strength of the traditional Bamana religion, and that its rules and prohibitions can prevail over Islam. The locking device consists of two pins, and the key insertion is superior. Brown patina. Provenance: Cercle of Bougouni (Bougouni).

69

Figure 28. H. 13½ in. (34.3 cm)

The vertical beam of this very old and well patinated lock is surmounted by a prominent neck and a male head devoid of external ears. This understated form, however, represents a male figure of prominence. The precise meaning of this lock cannot be deduced from its rudimentary form and the five horizontal panels of double-lined lozenges pyroengraved on its vertical beam. The horizontal beam appears to be a later replacement, and does not contain any surface engraving. This lock could represent a legendary hero, someone of special status, a notable ancestor, or else a man described in fables or myths. The lower end of the vertical beam is stylized into a recessed, anteriorly curving and inverted triangular form representing the head of the python. The locking device consists of two pins, and the key insertion is superior. Brown patina. Provenance: Cercle of Kolokani (Bélédougou).

Figure 29. H. 16 in. (40.7 cm)

The face of this unusual lock has been hollowed out into a deep, triangular cavity. Blacksmith informants in the Bélédougou stated that these cavities are *sélé dinw.* This term is also used to describe the small excavation that is made in the side wall at the base of a grave into which a body is placed. The cavity is then sealed up and the grave filled. Thus, the body rests not at the base of the grave, but off to the side of it. These cavities in locks recall similar ones made in the ritual block of wood called *Pembélé* that represents the original *Pembélé* described in the legend of creation. All these cavities are the domain of powerful spirits and the abode of the *nyama* (vital life powers, forces, or energies) of deceased ancestors. These cavities then project enormous protective powers. The vertical beam of this lock bears no surface engravings. However, in keeping with the *sélé din* symbolism of *Pemba*, the creator God, the right-hand side of the horizontal beam has two vertical rows of double-lined chevrons, representing *Pemba's* cosmic travels, the annual trajectory of the sun, and the orbit of Venus. An unusual feature of the horizontal beam is the presence of engraved, double-lined Xs on the top and bottom of the key insertion end. The locking device consists of two pins, and the key insertion is lateral. Gray and brown patina. Provenance: Cercle of Kolokani (Bélédougou).

70

Figure 30. H. 14½ in. (36.9 cm)

The precise meaning of this lock cannot be deduced from either its overall architectonics or from surface pyroengravings, which are lacking on both beams. The prominent neck and powerful head, devoid of external ears, project an imagery of strength needed to counter sorcery. This anti-sorcery theme is repeated in the recessed, anteriorly curving and inverted triangular form at the base of the vertical beam which represents the head of the python. The superior surface of the horizontal beam is covered with a protective metal sheath. The locking device consists of two pins, and the key insertion is superior. Black patina. Provenance: Cercle of Yanfolilla (Bougouni).

Figure 31. H. 13¾ in. (34.9 cm)

The surface decorations on the vertical beam of this lock consist of four panels of chevrons recalling the cosmic travels of *Faro* and *Mouso Koroni Koundyé*. The dominant head is sculpted as an anteroposterior arching form with a very reduced face at its lowermost point. The nasal septum is pierced with a hole, as are the posterior bases of the large, pointed, external ears. The face and forehead contain scarifications while the anterior surfaces of the neck and head are sculpted with excavated triangular shapes. The prominent ears recall the auditory powers of the *Kono* society, for the *Kono* hears everything. The facial scarifications and holes for ear and nose rings are not simply adornments, but also symbols of *Mouso Koroni Koundyé's* creative activities. The superior surface of the horizontal beam is covered by a protective strip of metal, partially eroded through use. The locking device consists of four pins, which is unusual, and the key insertion is lateral. Black patina. Provenance: Cercle of Dioila (Baninko).

BUTTERFLIES, SNAILS, OWLS, AND ORPHANS

Figure 32. H. 15½ in. (39.4 cm)

Extremely delicate in form, and lacking both depth and mass, this lock represents the butterfly (*mpérémpéréni*). According to legend, God originally created the butterfly as both a large and an important creature. However, overcome by pride and vanity, the butterfly offended God, who in turn reduced it to a small, light, and fragile creature. Thus, like *Mouso Koroni Koundyé*, who tried to be God's equal, the butterfly fell from favor. In this sense, the butterfly represents *Mouso Koroni* and her offenses against the creator God, *Pemba*. The butterfly is also connected to the python, because the Bamana see similarities in their physical movements. The head of this lock is surmounted by two symmetrical protuberances symbolizing the butterfly's wings. The nose and the tips of the wings are pierced with holes, which at one time may have contained rings of thread or beads, also symbols of *Mouso Koroni*. This simultaneous dual symbolism of *Mouso Koroni* and the butterfly is reflected in the human legs at one end of the vertical beam and wings at the other. The vertical beam is engraved with lozenges around three central rectangles, while the horizontal beam has panels of lozenges at either end. Of great importance, the vertical beam has three large, double-lined Xs whose upper and lower spaces are blackened through pyroengraving. When viewed on either the vertical or horizontal axis, these represent stylized butterfly wings. The superior surface of the horizontal beam is covered by a strip of metal. The locking device consists of two pins, and the key insertion is superior. Brown patina. Provenance: Cercle of Bamako (Djitoumou).

Figure 33. H. 14¼ in. (36.2 cm)

The snail (*kotè*), which is represented by this lock, has important meanings for the Bamana. It is the only animal with horns that cannot do any harm. The word *kotè* itself means "that which has no consequence," "that which does no harm." As such, it is intimately linked to the *Korè* initiation society which teaches men that they will undergo endless reincarnations. Initiates are subjected to a symbolic death which has no real physical consequences. This symbolic death is like the snail, inoffensive and incapable of causing physical harm. Because of its intimate connection to the *Korè* society, members are prohibited from eating snails. Sculpted in the image of a snail, this lock represents the *Korè* society and its beliefs and values. The lower portion of the vertical beam is sculpted in the form of a flare that represents *Faro* and his powers. Although surface graphic signs are sparse on this lock, they are located in unusual places on the vertical beam. The neck is encircled by single-lined lozenges which are also etched into the lateral sides of the horns. The horizontal beam is devoid of graphic signs. The designs on this lock appear to have been incised into the surface and not pyroengraved. The locking device consists of two pins, and the key insertion is lateral. Gray patina. Provenance: Cercle of Bamako (Djitoumou).

Figure 34. H. 14¼ in. (36.2 cm)

The head of this lock contains an inverted face and reversed ears, as well as the horns of the snail. When viewed upside down, the forehead is incised with four long, parallel lines that stretch to the base of the nose. The tip of the nose is pierced with a hole for the insertion of a thread or beaded ring, and the mouth is open. This reversal and inversion of essential anatomical parts of the head, along with the presence of the four scarifications and the open mouth, represent *Mouso Koroni Koundyé* and her disordered behavior. This is a female face, coded as such by the four scarifications, open mouth, and pierced nasal septum. The number four is female for the Bamana, while three is male. The prominence of the scarifications allude to *Mouso Koroni*, who invented them during the creation period. Thus, most of the symbolism of the lock's head refers to *Mouso Koroni*. Protruding from the top of the head are snail horns, which themselves are innocuous and which can cause no harm. This linking of snail horns to symbols of *Mouso Koroni* tells people that *Faro* finally subdued her, put an end to her disordered conduct, and rendered her harmless. This counterbalancing of *Faro's* powers and those of *Mouso Koroni* are etched on the vertical beam as opposing rows of chevrons along its length. These represent the complementary and antagonistic character of these two beings and the reverse character of their original travels. For *Mouso Koroni* traveled west-south-east-north, while *Faro* followed a path that took him east, west, south, and north. The superior surface of the horizontal beam is covered by a metal strip, which has been meticulously worked into perfectly aligned and elevated ridges that practically run its length. At the key insertion end of this strip, there are four similar vertical ridges on the metal. The face of the horizontal beam is etched with a large, single-lined central X flanked by double-lined Xs on either side. The locking device consists of two pins, and the key insertion is superior. Brown patina. Provenance: Cercle of Kolokani (Bélédougou).

Figure 35. H. 16¼ in. (41.3 cm)

The head of this lock is sculpted in the form of an owl. The various species of owls are known to the Bamana by slightly different names. These include *nguélou* and *gouélou* (owl), and *guinguin, guenguen* and *guingui* (hawk owl). Owls are greatly feared by the Bamana, who believe that night sorcerers (*soubaw*) can change themselves into owls, and as such can then become invisible. They enter houses at night, as a fine breath capable of traversing doors and walls. Their preferred victims are young girls, whose blood they drink. Locks were often sculpted in the form of owls in the Bélédougou, where this belief is strong. Informants there say that the sculpted figure of the owl reminds people of this danger, and also acts as an anti-sorcery agent. While the flare at the base of the vertical beam could represent an owl's tail, it could also symbolize that of the swallow (*nanalékou*). The swallow is *Faro's* aerial messenger, and symbolizes his power. There are no surface designs on this lock. However, both ends of the vertical beam are sculpted with depressed triangular forms. The upper inverted one represents the male principle, and the lower one the female. The locking device consists of two pins, and the key insertion is lateral. Black patina. Provenance: Arrondissement of Didiéni, Cercle of Kolokani (Bélédougou).

Figure 36. H. 15 in. (38.1 cm)

Like the previous lock, this one is also from the Arrondissement of Didiéni in the Cercle of Kolokani, which lies in the northern Bamana country. The head is sculpted in the form of an owl, but with hints of a human face. This insertion of anthropomorphic features is repeated at the base of the vertical beam by large human legs. The female principle is represented by a large, upright triangle carved into the upper portion of the vertical beam. Its counterpart, the male principle, is represented by a similar but inverted triangle at the base of the beam. The locations of these triangular depressions are the reverse of those on the previous lock. The horizontal beam bears no graphic signs, but its superior surface is covered by metal. The locking device consists of two pins, and the key insertion is superior. Black patina. Provenance: Arrondissement of Didiéni, Cercle of Kolokani (Bélédougou).

73

Figure 37. H. 15 in. (38.1 cm)

The depiction of bats (*ntonsow*), as in this lock, has no reference to the creation legend. Rather, bats represent for the Bamana an ambiguous creature that is neither bird nor animal. The well-known Bamana proverb, *Ntoso, i ma ke kono ye. Ntoso, i ma ke wara ye* (Bat, you are not a bird. Bat, you are not an animal), addresses ambiguous life situations in which people become confused about their beliefs and values, and have difficulty defining themselves. This is also a clear allusion to the erosive effects of Islam on the traditional Bamana way of life (*Bamanaya*), and the confusion and ambiguities inherent in syncretism. Thus, from one perspective, the sculpted image of the bat reminds people to remain faithful to *Bamanaya* so as to avoid ambiguities in their beliefs and values. The bat also serves as a bridge between man and the world of animals, and in so doing draws attention to the fact that humans must connect the extremes in their own lives. Although there are no surface designs on this lock, nails and metal disks were used to create eyes. The face is naturalistic and has an open mouth. The locking device consists of two pins, and the key insertion is lateral. Brown patina. Provenance: Cercle of Kolokani (Bélédougou).

Figure 38. H. 14 in. (35.6 cm)

Unlike the previous figure, this lock presents a more abstract rendering of the bat. It also incorporates key anthropomorphic features such as a human neck and legs. The lobes of the ears are pierced, as is the nasal septum, which in the past may have contained decorative threads or strings of beads. The horizontal beam is missing, but the vertical one contains four sequential, multilined Xs arrayed along the vertical axis. The locking device consists of two pins. Black patina. Provenance: Cercle of Koulikoro (Bélédougou).

Figure 39. H. 16½ in. (42 cm)

This unusual lock represents a smoking pipe (*taba da*) which is intended as a rebuke to Islam and its adherents, and as affirming the values of the traditional Bamana way of life (*Bamanaya*). It declares that smoking tobacco is a poor replacement for drinking millet beer (*dolo*). Alcohol consumption is prohibited by Islam whose clerics in Mali often advise recent converts to use tobacco instead. There are several fables in the Bamana country recounting how prominent traditionalists converted to Islam and then unsuccessfully tried to substitute tobacco use for alcohol consumption. They invariably abandoned Islam, returned to their traditional Bamana way of life, and had locks sculpted in the form of pipes to document their experiences. These locks represent an affirmation of the traditional Bamana way of life and a rejection of Islam. The vertical beam of this lock contains four sequential, multi-lined Xs and a group of seven horizontal lines at the base representing *Pemba*, the creator God. The horizontal beam bears groups of lozenges at either end, while the front and rear edges of the key insertion hole are scalloped. A metal sheet covers the superior surface of the horizontal beam. The locking device consists of two pins, and the key insertion is superior. Black patina. Provenance: Cercle of Bamako (Djitoumou).

Figure 40. H. 17½ in. (44.5 cm)

This lock represents the social situation of an orphan (*fala*). In traditional Bamana society, orphans were completely devoid of all familial connections, and were thus suspected of having an evil character (*tere*). For the Bamana, the *tere* is a powerful spiritual element that at death becomes *nyama*, a vital life power, force, or energy. Because orphans were greatly feared, they were exiled from their own villages and held responsible for the death of their parents. Locks of this type appear to have originated in Bougouni, where a well-known fable recounts the tribulations of an orphan. Continuously rejected by society, he decided to wear a collar made of several hoops of twisted vegetable fiber. Such collars (*krin krin*) are usually worn by hunting dogs, and make a scraping sound whenever the animals move. Equating himself with a dog, he entered a village where he sang of his being a victim of social injustice before the house of the chief. Moved by this sad tale, the chief defied both convention and public opinion, and adopted the orphan. Locks such as this one commemorate this fable, of which there are several versions. The head of the lock is highly abstract, with incised vertical lines of Xs on the two central triangular forms. The *krin krin* is represented by three rectangular forms, one of which is below the neck, and two of which are above it. The anterior surface of the vertical beam is incised with fourteen rows of interdigitated, double-lined chevrons aligned on the horizontal axis. An unusual feature is the presence of double-lined Xs along the sides of the upper portion of the vertical beam. The horizontal beam is devoid of surface designs. The locking device consists of two pins, and the key insertion is lateral. Black and brown patina. Provenance: Cercle of Bougouni (Bougouni).

75

Figure 41. H. 12½ in. (31.8 cm)

The head of this lock incorporates both anthropomorphic and zoomorphic features. The long face resembles the snout of a baboon (*gon koro*), while the small open mouth and the forehead are clearly human. Although not very large, this lock has an inherent mass that conveys a sense of strength and power. Of significance is the unusual insertion of the attachment nails through the base of the neck and the terminal flare at the base of the vertical beam. The surfaces of both beams are devoid of designs. The precise meaning of this lock cannot be deduced from its architectonics alone. The locking device consists of two pins, and the key insertion is lateral. Black patina. Provenance: Cercle of Bamako (Djitoumou).

TORTOISES, LIZARDS, AND CROCODILES

Figure 42. H. 12 in. (30.5 cm)

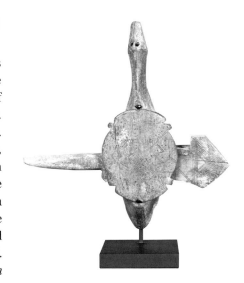

Locks depicting the tortoise (*koro kara*) are relatively rare. This well-preserved example was probably affixed to an interior door, given its patina and overall fine condition. For the Bamana, the shell of the tortoise not only protects its body, but also symbolizes protection of a family's material and spiritual well-being. As such, it also protects a family from sorcery. Tortoises are also avatars of *Faro*. The vertical beam is richly engraved with graphic signs. These include double-lined chevrons on the snout, rectangles on the neck, and gouged-out, small triangles on the neck and carapace. The carapace is almost whimsically decorated with a large, triple-lined X, double-lined chevrons, lozenges, and small, gouged-out triangles. The eyes of the tortoise are represented on the head by two adjacent deep holes which create a sense of watchfulness. The horizontal beam, whose superior surface is covered by a protective metal strip, is richly engraved with double-lined Xs, parallel vertical lines, lozenges, and gouged-out triangles. The locking device contains three pins, and the key insertion is lateral. Illustrated in Bamana Door Locks. *African Arts* 1974, V(3):52–56, 84, and in *African Art in American Collections*. Washington and London: Smithsonian Institution Press, 1989, 537. Gray patina. Provenance: Cercle of Dioila (Baninko).

Figure 43. H. 13 in. (33 cm)

Locks mounted on posts such as this one were once common in the eastern Bamana country. The posts were inserted into the floor of a house or vestibule adjacent to the door. The tapered end of the horizontal beam of the lock slides across the inner, lower surface of the door, thereby securing it. These locks can be opened and closed from the outside with a key by inserting one's hand through a large hole made through the wall. This lock is unique in that its sculptor and approximate time of creation are known. It was sculpted by Siriman Fané, a master sculptor from the village of Koké in the Arrondissement of Markala, Cercle of Segou, in the early 1930s. Siriman later gained renown as a master sculptor of marionettes. This lock was ordered by Sidiki Sanogo of the nearby Marka village of Boussin, and used by him and his wife, Assiou Sanogo, to lock the door that gave access to their vestibule (*blo*). Sidiki Sanogo was a fervent Moslem, as was his son, Mahamoutou Sanogo. Mahamoutou Sanogo and his wife, Mandieni Sougoulé, continued to use the lock until the mid-1960s. The lock had been in disuse for a few years when Mamoutou and his son, Amadou Sanogo, gave it to this writer in 1970. I showed it to Siriman Fané, who remembered sculpting it, and said that he had fashioned it to represent the large water iguana (*kana*), a powerful anti-sorcery image. He pointed to the stylized cleft at the base of the triangular form, and said: "This is the open mouth of the *kana* by which it can seize sorcerers. The *kana* is *Faro*, and *Faro* is the *kana*." In making the last statement, Siriman meant that the *kana* is an avatar of *Faro*. He also said: "The *kana* eats the *sirantoula* (gecko)." This statement has enormous meaning because the Bamana greatly fear the small, gray gecko, believing it to be nefarious, poisonous, and capable of causing leprosy. They believe that when a sorcerer places a gecko in someone's food or bed, it can lead to that person developing leprosy. There are no surface designs on the vertical beam, while the horizontal beam bears only three sets of vertical lines. The locking device consists of three pins, and the key insertion is lateral. Natural blond-colored wood. Provenance: Sculpted by Siriman Fané in the village of Koké in the early 1930s, and used by members of the Sanogo Family in the village of Boussin, Arrondissement of Markala, Cercle of Segou (Segou).

Figure 44. H. 19 in. (48.3 cm)

This lock was sculpted in the late 1930s by master sculptor Siriman Fané of the village of Koké. According to Siriman, it was intended to represent the *kana* (water iguana), and to protect against sorcerers and malevolent *nyama*. The triangular lizard head sits atop a stylized neck, while the vertical beam is supported by two legs. These anthropomorphic features, according to Siriman, reflect *Faro's* possession of some human physical characteristics. Their contextual association with the stylized form of a *kana* emphasizes the intimate relationship between *Faro* and these water creatures; they can serve as his avatars, and are empowered to neutralize sorcerers. Some of the architectonics of this lock, such as the long, dangling legs, resemble those of some marionettes sculpted by Siriman. This lock was made for a family in the village of Miniankabougou in the Arrondissement of Markala, Cercle of Segou, who discarded it in the late 1960s after having converted to Islam. There are no pyroengraved designs on either beam of this lock. The locking device consists of two pins, and the key insertion is lateral. Brown patina. Provenance: Sculpted by Siriman Fané in the village of Koké in the late 1930s for use in the village of Miniankabougou, Arrondissement of Markala, Cercle of Segou (Segou).

Figure 45. H. 16 in. (40.6 cm)

This lock was originally mounted on a post, and not attached to a door. Like the lock in Figure 43, it was used on the interior of a house or vestibule, and its locking mechanism was accessed through a hole in the lower wall. Representing the *kana* (water iguana), its vertical beam is crowned with the slender neck and head of the iguana, and two stylized protuberances represent the front legs. A large, double-lined X covers the center of the vertical beam, and is flanked above and below by three rows of double-lined Xs. This powerful fertility symbol is repeated on the anterior surface of the neck and the base of the head, while the anterior surface of the snout contains double-lined chevrons, reflecting the cosmic travels of the supernatural beings and symbolizing the solar year. The surfaces of the protuberances are covered with diagonal lines, eroded on the lateral aspects, representing *Pemba* and his divinity. The locking device consists of five pins. Natural blond-colored wood. Provenance: Cercle of Segou (Segou).

CATALOGUE

Figure 46. H. 18 in. (45.7 cm)

The *koro* (land iguana) is a large lizard with a snout that is not as long as that of the *kana* (water iguana). The true-to-life head of this lock, divided by a central vertical ridge, is complemented by the naturalistic treatment given to the vertical beam which is anteriorly rounded into three equal parallel sections, separated by ridges. A short tail is represented at the base of the vertical beam by an anteriorly curving form capped by an inverted pyramid. Like the *kana*, the *koro* is a powerful anti-sorcery symbol. Given its large size, it is capable of destroying the small gray gecko (*sirantoula*) that is believed to be a sorcery agent. There are no pyroengraved designs on this lock. The locking device consists of two pins, and the key insertion is lateral. Black patina. Provenance: Cercle of Bamako (Djitoumou).

Figure 47. H. 18¾ in. (47.6 cm)

The head of the *koro* lizard has been sculpted realistically in this lock, as in Figure 46. It is anteriorly separated into two halves by a vertical ridge. While the horizontal beam is devoid of graphic signs, the vertical one contains large, triple-lined Xs in its superior and inferior portions surrounding a central panel dominated by a triple-lined lozenge and partial lozenges. The inferior extremity of the vertical beam is stylized into a recessed, anteriorly curving, and inverted triangular shape representing the head of the python. The horizontal beam's superior surface is covered by a protective metal sheath. The locking device consists of two pins, and the key insertion is superior. Black patina. Provenance: Cercle of Bougouni (Bougouni).

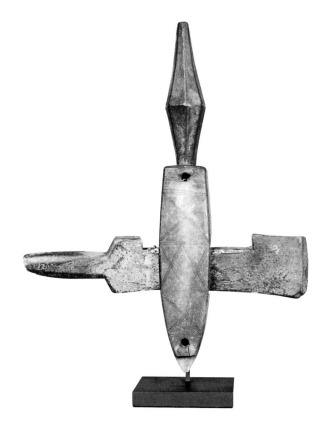

Figure 48. H. 18¾ in. (47.6 cm)

The water iguana (*kana*) is rendered in this lock by a massive vertical beam whose surface is divided into sections by ridges. Termite damage and erosion have obliterated some of these features. The surface of the head is divided into four sections by ridges, the central one being scalloped. At the base of the vertical beam is a fish tail, evoking the *kana's* association with water, the abode of *Faro*. The anterior surface of the horizontal beam is almost completely eroded. The locking device consists of two pins, and the key insertion is superior. Brown patina and surface erosion. Provenance: Cercle of Koulikoro (Bélédougou).

Figure 49. H. 24 in. (61 cm)

The *kana* (water iguana) is depicted realistically in this large lock. The vertical beam, which is configured in the form of a lizard, is engraved with chevrons representing *Faro's* early cosmic travels, the annual trajectory of the sun, and Venus' yearly course. These chevrons are configured on the body so as to form central lozenges over the back. Eleven sequential vertical chevrons cover the tail. Although the horizontal beam is devoid of surface engravings, its ends are sculpted in bold anterior relief from the rest of the beam. The locking device contains two pins, and the key insertion is lateral. Brown patina. Provenance: Cercle of Bamako (Djitoumou).

Figure 50. H. 26¼ in. (66.7 cm)

From the village of Koiyo in the Cercle of Kolokani (Bélédougou), this large lock is configured in the realistic form of the *kana* (water iguana). The head is engraved with lozenges while the neck, body, and tail are decorated with chevrons arranged along the vertical axis across the spine. The key insertion in the horizontal beam is lateral and its anterior surface is covered by lozenges. The other end of the horizontal beam is covered by a double-lined X and lozenges. The locking device contains two pins. Brown patina. Provenance: Village of Koiyo, Cercle of Kolokani (Bélédougou).

Figure 51. H. 44 in. (111.8 cm)

Remarkable for the length of its vertical beam, this lock represents the *kana* (water iguana). Besides protecting people from sorcery, the *kana* symbolizes fertility, wealth, and good fortune. Its tail and that of the *koro* (land iguana) symbolize the immature penis of a young boy. This lock lacks the horizontal beam, and has no surface engravings. The locking device contains two pins. Brown patina. Provenance: Cercle of Koulikoro (Bélédougou).

Figure 52. H. 17 in. (43.2 cm)

The *bama* (crocodile) has several powerful symbolic meanings for the Bamana. It is a symbol of the *Korè* initiation society, a mount for village protector spirits (*dassiri*), and the guardian of *Faro's* waters. This mythical crocodile was the first to stow away the ark of creation in *Faro's* pond, and thus is in close relationship with this deity. It follows that the crocodile is a potent force against sorcery. The head of the vertical beam of this lock is realistically rendered into that of the crocodile. Although neither beam contains any surface engravings, the lower end of the vertical one is configured into a recessed, anteriorly inclined and inverted triangle representing the head of the python. The superior surface of the vertical beam is covered with a protective strip of metal. The locking device contains two pins, and the key insertion is superior. Brown patina. Provenance: Cercle of Bamako (Djitoumou).

Figure 53. H. 17 in. (43.8 cm)

The head of the crocodile is rendered realistically in this lock. The vertical beam is richly pyroengraved with a large, central, double-lined X, flanked by two panels of double-lined lozenges. The inferior pole of the vertical beam is configured into the abstract form of a python's head. The horizontal beam contains closely arranged diagonal lines on its left end, symbolizing *Pemba's* divinity, and more widely spaced similar but double lines on the right, emblems of all that *Pemba* confided to *Faro*. The center of the horizontal beam is covered by a large, triple-lined X. The locking device contains one pin, and the key insertion is superior. Brown patina. Provenance: Cercle of Kolondieba (Bougouni).

DOORS

Figure 54. Door: H. 51 in. x W. 26¾ in. (129.5 cm x 67.9 cm)

Lock: H. 15½ in. (39.4 cm)

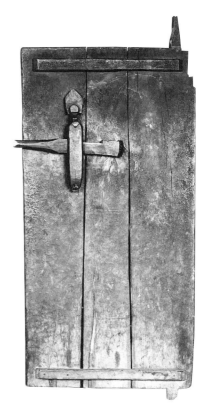

This exterior house door consists of three wooden panels held together by upper and lower wooden crossbars, and by four indigenously forged internal metal dowels. The upper hinge is cylindrical in shape, tapers toward the top, measures 5 inches (12.7 cm) in length. The lower hinge is 2.5 inches (6.35 cm) long, and is slightly broader. The upper lateral edge of the right panel is sculpted in a step-like pattern. The door shows signs of extensive weathering, as well as use and encrustation patina. The vertical beam of the lock depicts a highly stylized *bamada* hat, a featureless face, and a prominent neck. The lower end of the vertical beam is sculpted in the form of a recessed, inverted triangle symbolizing the python's head. There is no pyroengraving on either beam. The superior surface of the horizontal beam is covered by a strip of protective metal. The locking device consists of two pins, and the key insertion is superior. Black and gray patina. Provenance: Village of Tamala, Arrondissement of Quélessébougou, Cercle of Bamako (Djitoumou).

Figure 55.
Door: H. 56 in. x W. 27 in. (142.2 cm x 68.6 cm)

Lock: H. 19 in. (48.3 cm)

Consisting of two wooden panels of unequal width, this exterior house door is held together by upper and lower wooden crossbars, and by two indigenously forged metal dowels. The right panel is much wider than the left one, as is often the case with two-paneled doors. This is because the wider right panel with the finial hinges is better able to support the lighter and narrower left-sided one. The original lower hinge either wore down or broke off. An extensively worn replacement hinge is attached by indigenously smelted nails to the posterior surface of the right lower corner of the door. The upper cylindrical hinge measures 3¼ inches (8.3 cm) in length, while the lower rectangular one is 2¾ inches (7.0 cm) long. The door shows signs of extensive weathering, as well as use and encrustation patina. The vertical beam of the lock depicts the abstract form of the crocodile's jaws as two horn-like structures coming up from the sides of the head. The prominent neck symbolizes the *Komo's* knowledge and power to teach. The lower end of the vertical beam is sculpted in the form of a recessed, anteriorly curving and inverted triangle symbolizing the python's head. The anterior surface of the vertical beam is engraved with four panels of double-lined Xs. The horizontal beam has no surface engravings, but its superior surface is covered by a strip of protective metal. The locking device consists of two pins, and the key insertion is superior. Black and gray patina. Provenance: Village of Kéléya, Arrondissement of Kéléya, Cercle of Bougouni (Bougouni).

Figure 56.   Door: H. 51½ in. x W. 26 in. (130.8 cm x 66.0 cm)

Lock: H. 17¼ in. (43.8 cm)

The three panels of this extremely old exterior house door are held together by four indigenously forged internal metal dowels and by a superior wooden crossbar whose inferior edge is scalloped. The bar is attached to the panels by traditionally smelted nails. The lower portion of the door shows surface signs of the presence of a former crossbar. The hinges at either extremity of the right side show extensive use. The upper hinge is sculpted in the form of an inverted cone, and measures 3¼ inches (8.3 cm) in length, while the lower cylindrical cone is 3½ inches (8.9 cm) long. The central and upper portions of this door show evidence of extensive use and encrustation patina. The latter derive not only from use, but also from sacrificial offerings intended to provide protection from sorcery. The vertical beam of the lock depicts a male figure with a stylized *bamada* hat and prominent neck, symbols of the anti-sorcery powers of the *Komo* and its knowledge. The lock as well as adjacent areas of the door are heavily worn and covered with many layers of encrustation. Thus, any possible original surface engravings have been obliterated. The locking device consists of two pins, and the key insertion is superior. Black and gray patina. Provenance: Village of Tamala, Arrondissement of Quélessébougou, Cercle of Bamako (Djitoumou).

Figure 57. Door: H. 50½ in. x W. 25 in. (128.3 cm x 63.5 cm) Lock: H. 14¾ in. (37.5 cm)

Doors with sculpted surfaces are extremely rare among the Bamana. This sculpted door consists of two panels of unequal width held together by two indigenously forged internal metal dowels and four indigenously made external U-shaped metal brackets. The U-shaped brackets were driven through the wood, and the ends of one folded over on the anterior surface of the door. A similar locally made U-shaped metal bracket was driven through the posterior surface of the upper portion of the right plank in order to stabilize a crack. All brackets show signs of extreme age and patinization. The upper hinge at the top of the right plank measures 4½ inches (11.4 cm), and consists of a cylindrical post atop a right-angled triangular form. It exhibits signs of extensive use patina. On Bamana doors, the lower hinge often wears down because it bears most of the weight. The original lower hinge on this door wore down and was replaced by one attached posteriorly by two nails first driven through the right lower anterior corner. Although this replacement hinge is lost, the indigenously forged nails remain. The anterior surface of the door is sculpted with three rows of chevrons and five iguanas. The upper and lower lines each contain seventeen chevrons, while the middle one contains nineteen. These lines of chevrons recall the cosmic travels of *Mouso Koroni Koundyé* and *Faro*, the diurnal and annual movements of the sun, and the annual path of Venus. The wider right panel is sculpted with a vertical row of three water iguanas (*kanaw*), whose surfaces are incised with horizontal lines. The lengths of these stylized lizards are respectively, from top to bottom: 12 inches (30.5 cm), 11 inches (27.9 cm), and 13 inches (33.0 cm). The left panel is sculpted with two similar iguanas, the top one measuring 12 inches (30.5 cm) in length, and the bottom one 12½ inches (31.8 cm). The *kana* is an avatar of *Faro*, and a powerful anti-sorcery symbol. The lock on this door depicts a woman with flexed forearms holding conical breasts, a prominent umbilicus, and long legs. While the vertical beam does not contain any graphic signs, the horizontal one is incised with a large, double-lined X over its center. A series of single-lined lozenges is present on the left, and double-lined lozenges on the right end beneath the scalloped opening for the key insertion. The fertility symbolism of this lock is communicated by the prominent breasts, which are held up by the hands with which they are fused and by the lozenges which represent seminal and amniotic fluids. The superior surface of the horizontal beam is covered by a protective metal strip. The locking device contains two pins, and the key insertion is superior.

The small, rectangular area of wear patina on the left plank just above the lock's horizontal beam may have been due to rubbing from the more superiorly placed beam of a previous lock. This door was originally used in the family compound (*goua*) of the Coulibaly family of blacksmiths (*numuw*) in the village of Sienbougou, and was discarded in the early 1970s. Exhibited in *Icon and Symbol. The Cult of the Ancestor in African Art.* Bloomfield Hills, Michigan: Cranbrook Academy of Art/ Museum, 1975, and in *Detroit Collects African Art.* Detroit, Michigan: Detroit Institute of Arts, 1977. Illustrated in *Icon and Symbol. The Cult of the Ancestor in African Art.* Bloomfield Hills, Michigan: Cranbrook Academy of Art/Museum, 1975, 6. Weathered, encrusted, and varied brown usc patina. Provenance: Village of Sienbougou, Arrondissement of Kéléya, Cercle of Bougouni (Bougouni).

DOGON LOCKS

The Dogon people, who live to the east of the Bamana, also use sculpted locks on house, granary, and sanctuary doors. The overall sculptural forms of these locks, as well as their pyroengraved surface designs, reflect Dogon legends, religious beliefs, cosmology, and social themes. The vertical and horizontal beams of Dogon locks are often wider than Bamana ones, the locking pins more numerous and of narrower diameter, and the key insertion lateral. The keys are usually wooden with metal teeth corresponding to the locking pins. The following five locks shown depict twin figures or structures atop the vertical beams. Although similar, these figures symbolize different aspects of Dogon legend and religious belief.

Figure 58. H. 10¾ ln. (27.3 cm)

This lock represents the twins of *Binu Seru*, a Dogon ancestor. His wife gave birth to the first set of twins, one male and one female. The twins of *Binu Seru* are often depicted without facial features or with the male as having a triangular face and the female a square one. The latter physical characteristics are present in this lock. Brown patina. Provenance: Cercle of Bandiagara (Kambari).

Figure 59. H. 13¾ in. (34.9 cm)

Faceless figures such as those depicted on this lock represent either the twins of *Binu Seru* or *Nommo* pairs. The *Nommo* were human-like beings created when *Amma*, the supreme creative force, had intercourse with the earth. Green in color and serpent-like below the waist, these beings gave birth to the original Dogon ancestors. Illustrated in Dogon Door Locks. *African Arts* 1978, XI(4):54–57, 96. Brown patina. Provenance: Arrondissement of Kendié, Cercle of Bandiagara (N'duléri).

Figure 60. H. 18 in. (45.7 cm)

The twin figures atop this large lock could represent either a *Nommo* pair or *Tellem* twins. The latter, according to legends, were either dwarfs or giants who inhabited the Bandiagara Cliffs before the Dogon arrived. Black patina. Provenance: Cercle of Bankass (Seno-Barassara).

Figure 61. H. 15 in. (38.1 cm)

This very old and beautiful lock may portray the twins of *Amma Seru*, another early Dogon ancestor. However, some informants see a *Nommo* pair in the two seated figures. Illustrated in Dogon Door Locks. *African Arts* 1978, XI(4):54–57,96. Weathered gray patina. Provenance: Village of Irieli, Arrondissement of Sanga, Cercle of Bandiagara (Bambou).

Figure 62. H. 18¾ in. (47.6 cm)

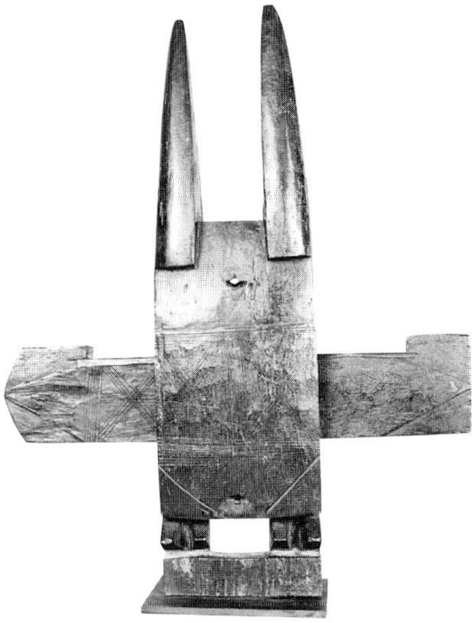

The pointed, horn-like structures atop this lock could represent stylized *Nommo* figures or the horns of the roan antelope (*ka*). If the symbolism is the latter, the lock would have been used on the door of a *Binu* sanctuary granary. The *Binu* cult links the living to those early ancestors who are immortal. Locks of this type, representing the roan antelope, are used on the *Binu* sanctuary granaries of families for whom the animal is a totem. Illustrated in Dogon Door Locks. *African Arts* 1978, XI(4):54–57, 96. Black patina. Provenance: Cercle of Bankass (Seno-Barassara).

The five Dogon locks shown here represent a variety of themes.

Figure 63. H. 8½ in. (21.6 cm)

Locks of this type sculpted with ostriches (*ogotanala*) are often used on the doors of *Lébé* sanctuaries. *Lébé* was the first *hogon* (priest-chief) of the Dogon who was a descendant of the eighth *Nommo*. He was eaten by the seventh *Nommo* and their life forces mingled. The seventh *Nommo* then vomited, and a new *Lébé* emerged, part human and part supernatural. This man-god eventually metamorphosed into a snake, and introduced death to the world. It is in the form of a snake that *Lébé* is believed to exist today. He visits the *hogons*, licks their bodies, and in so doing gives them and all humanity the strength to live. For the Dogon, *Lébé* is the mainspring of germination, the source of vital life force, and the protector of placentas. The Dogon honor *Lébé* with a cult and shrines. The latter often have locks on which ostriches are depicted. The ostrich is known for its zigzag course when running. This zigzagging is symbolic of *Lébé* the serpent because it replicates his movements. Thus, the ostrich is an avatar of *Lébé*. This bird's movements are also similar to those of the *Nommo* as they fell to earth in the form of rain. An ostrich egg is often present in a *hogon's* sanctuary, symbolizing *Lébé*. Illustrated in Dogon Door Locks. *African Arts* 1978; XI(4):54–57, 96. Brown patina. Provenance: Arrondissement of Ningari, Cercle of Bandiagara (N'duléri).

Figure 64. H. 12½ in. (31.8 cm)

This lock depicts a *hogon* on horseback. The *hogons* are the spiritual and temporal leaders of the Dogon, and play a key role in mediating disputes, dispensing justice, counteracting sorcery, and maintaining the delicate relationship between man and a pantheon of ancestral and nature spirits. Locks depicting riders represent not just a *hogon*, but also *Lébé*, the first *hogon*. As such, they are usually affixed to the *hogon's* door. Illustrated in Dogon Door Locks. *African Arts* 1978; XI(4):54-57, 96. Brown patina. Provenance: Arrondissement of Kendié, Cercle of Bandiagara (N'duléri).

Figure 65. H. 17 in. (43.2 cm)

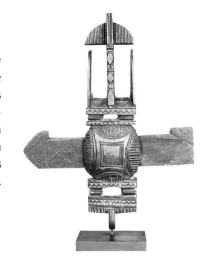

This elaborate lock combines the symbolism of the water tortoise (*kiru*) in the lower portion of the vertical beam and a hitching post (*so pegu*) and what appears to be roan antelope (*ka*) horns in the upper part. The water tortoise is symbolic of the placenta of the *Nommo*, and locks with this unique figure are often affixed to the granaries holding the harvest of a *hogon's* fields. Locks depicting the water tortoise are also affixed to the granary doors of women who capture these reptiles in the bush and keep them in their compounds for purification rites. These rites are associated with the postpartum period and menstruation. According to some informants, the antelope horns could be either totemic representations of the roan antelope or else highly stylized *Nommo* figures. Deep brown patina. Provenance: Cercle of Bankass (Seno-Barassara).

Figure 66. H. 16½ in. (41.9 cm)

The simple architectonics of this lock may have several meanings. The semicircular form atop the vertical beam represents a hitching post (*so pegu*). However, some informants stated that it could also be a *Nommo* figure, given the two breast-like protuberances on the anterior surface of the neck. It may also represent the person of the individual who owns a horse. Locks that represent hitching posts are affixed to granary doors where a horse's feed is stored. Among the Dogon, anyone wealthy enough to own a horse can also afford to construct a separate granary for its feed. Illustrated in Dogon Door Locks. *African Arts* 1978, XI(4):54–57, 96. Gray patina. Provenance: Cercle of Bankass (Seno-Barassara).

Figure 67. H. 19½ in. (49.5 cm)

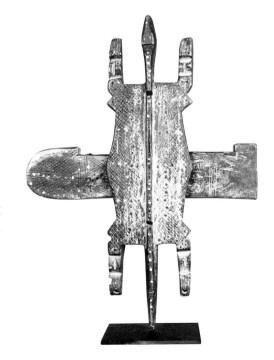

The architectonics of this lock contain the structural elements of both lizards (*geo*) and crocodiles (*ayo*). These two reptiles are frequently represented in locks. The lizard in locks symbolizes the prepuce of a circumcised boy's penis. The Dogon believe that the female element of a boy's spiritual being resides in his prepuce. On removal at the time of circumcision, it is transformed into a reddish-colored lizard that the Dogon call the sun lizard. The crocodile is also a common form on locks, and represents the animal that once belonged to the ancestor *Binu Seru*. Locks depicting crocodiles are frequently used by the totemic priests of the *Binu* cult for sealing granaries containing millet harvested from their fields. The close association of such locks with vital food supplies harvested from *Binu* fields means that they also symbolize *Binu Seru* himself. Illustrated in Dogon Door Locks. *African Arts* 1978, XI(4):54–57, 96. Gray patina. Provenance: Arrondissement of Wau, Cercle of Bandiagara (Seno-Barassara).

CATALOGUE

BWA LOCKS

The Bwa are a Voltaic people who live in southeastern Mali in the administrative cercles of Djenné, Koutiala, San, and Yorosso. They also live in the adjacent areas of Burkina Faso. Sharing a number of cultural commonalities with their neighbors, the Bobo, they are themselves sometimes referred to as the Bobo-Ulé. The Bwa are also related to the Dogon, and like them have strongly resisted the inroads of Islam. Bwa locks resemble a number of their Dogon counterparts in terms of overall structure, locking devices, and superficial, pyroengraved symbols. The latter include multi-lined Xs and multi-lined lozenges.

Figure 68. H. 18½ in. (47.0 cm)

The vertical beam of this lock is surmounted by a male head with a beard resting atop two prominent and laterally curving stylized breasts. The face is naturalistic with broad nares, an open mouth, and sloping forehead. A unique feature is the piece of wood sculpted to cover precisely the entire posterior surface of the vertical beam. This is rectangular in shape and pyroengraved with four successive panels from top to bottom that consist of double-lined Xs, double-lined lozenges, a quadruple-lined X crossed by a vertical triple line, and finally double-lined lozenges. The lower portion of the vertical beam is posteriorly recessed and horizontally incised across its center with a deep gouged-out line surrounded by two sets of pyroengraved lines. The horizontal beam has two panels of double-lined lozenges at either end. These graphic signs are similar to those found on both Bamana and Dogon locks. However, their precise meaning in a Bwa context cannot be assumed to be either the same or similar. Of note is the presence of a large, multilined X on the center of the vertical beam, vertically transected by a triple line, the symbol of the *Komo* among the Bamana. Brown patina. Provenance: Cercle of Bankass (Seno-Barassara).

Figure 69. H. 14½ in. (36.8 cm)

This lock, like the previous one, has a rectangular form, but it also has the characteristics of a statue, with its distinct head, legs, and feet. The facial features of the head are Dogon-like, especially the nose and chin. However, the five planes of the head are configured as rectangles, and meet almost at right angles, representing a form distinct from Bamana and Dogon sculpture. The forehead is crisscrossed with pyroengraved lines, and the neck is delicately and uniquely configured on all four sides by two mirror-image, trapezoidal forms. The vertical beam has two panels of engravings separated by a rectangular umbilicus, which itself bears a double-lined X. The upper panel consists of triple-lined lozenges, while the lower panel bears two adjacent quadruple-lined Xs. The horizontal beam has double-lined lozenges at either end. Unlike the previous Bwa lock, this one has legs with angular knees. However, the horizontal beam is similar in that it terminates with a spearhead-like locking end. Brown patina. Provenance: Cercle of Bankass (Seno-Barassara).

BIBLIOGRAPHY

Aherne, Tavey D. *Nakunte Diarra. Bogolanfini Artist of the Beledougou.* Bloomington: Indiana University Art Museum, 1992.

Arnoldi, Mary Jo. *Bamana and Bozo Puppetry of the Segou Region Youth Societies.* West Lafayette, Indiana: Department of Creative Arts, Purdue University, 1977.

———. Performance, Style and the Assertion of Identity in Malian Puppet Drama. *Journal of Folklore Research* 1988, 25(1–2):87–100.

———. *Playing with Time. Art and Performance in Central Mali.* Bloomington and Indianapolis: Indiana University Press, 1995.

———. Regional Puppet Theatre in Segu, Mali. *The Puppetry Journal* 1981, 32(4):14–19.

——— and Ezra, Kate. *Sama Ba.* The Elephant in Bamana Art. In *Elephant. The Animal and Its Ivory in African Culture.* Edited by Doran H. Ross. Los Angeles: Fowler Museum of Cultural History/University of California, 1992, 99–111.

Balesi, Charles John. *From Adversaries to Comrades-in-Arms: West Africans and the French Military, 1885–1918.* Waltham, MA: Crossroads Press, 1979.

Barry, Rahim Danto. *Portes d'Afrique.* Paris: Norma Editions, 1999.

Bazin, Msgr. H. *Dictionnaire Bambara-Français.* Paris: Imprimerie Nationale, 1906.

Berhaut, Jean. *Flore du Sénégal.* Second Edition. Dakar: Editions Clairafrique, 1967.

Berna, Beppe. *Porte & Serrature Dogon & Bambara. Selezionate da: Denise e Beppe Berna.* Bologna: Galleria del Vicolo Quartirolo, 1980.

Brasseur, Gérard. *Les Etablissements humains au Mali.* Dakar: Institut Fondamental d'Afrique Noire (IFAN), 1968.

Brasseur, Paule. *Bibliographie générale du Mali.* Dakar: Université de Dakar—Institut Français d'Afrique Noire (IFAN), 1964.

———. *Bibliographie générale du Mali* (1961–1970). Dakar: Université de Dakar—Institut Fondamental d'Afrique Noire (IFAN), 1976.

Brett-Smith, Sarah C. *The Making of Bamana Sculpture. Creativity and Gender.* Cambridge: Cambridge University Press, 1994.

———. The Poisonous Child. *RES: Anthropology and Aesthetics* 1983, 6:47–64.

———. Symbolic Blood. Cloths for Excised Women. *RES: Anthropology and Aesthetics* 1982, 3:15–31.

Brun, Joseph. Le totémisme chez quelques peuples du Soudan Occidental. *Anthropos* 1910, 5:843–869.

Calame-Griaule, Geneviève, Dupuis, Annie, and Ndiayé, Francine. *Serrures Dogon. Approche ethnomorphologique.* Paris: Département d'Afrique Noire, Laboratoire d'Ethnologie, Musée de l'Homme, 1976 (microfiche).

Cissé, Youssouf Tata. *Boli*, Statues et statuettes dans la religion Bambara. In *Magies.* Edited by Christiane Falgayrettes-Leveau, Suzanne Preston Blier, Youssouf Tata Cissé, Vincent Bouloré, and Arthur Bourgeois. Paris: Editions Dapper, 1996, 149-173.

Colleyn, Jean-Paul. *Les Chemins de Nya. Culte de possession au Mali.* Paris: Editions de l'Ecole des Hautes Etudes en Sciences Sociales, 1988.

——— and De Clippel, Catherine. *Bamanaya. Un' arte de vivere in Mali/Un art de vivre au Mali.* Milan: Centro Studi Archeologia Africana, 1998.

Conrad, David C. and Frank, Barbara E. *Status and Identity in West Africa. Nyamakalaw of Mande.* Bloomington: Indiana University Press, 1995.

Cordell, Dennis D., Gregory, Joel W., and Piché, Victor. *Hoe and Wage. A Social History of a Circular Migration System in West Africa.* Boulder, CO: Westview Press, 1998.

de Ganay, Solange. Aspects de mythologie et de symbolique Bambara. J*ournal de Psychologie Normale et Pathologique* 1949; 42:181–201.

———. Graphies Bambara des nombres. J*ournal de la Société des Africanistes* 1950; 20:295–305.

———. Une graphie soudanaise du doit du Createur. *Revue de l'Histoire des Religions* 1951; 139:45–49.

———. II. Graphies de voyages mythiques chez les Bambara. *Africa* 1951; 21:20–23.

Delafosse, Maurice. *Haut-Sénégal-Niger.* Tome I. *Le Pays, les Peuples, les Langues.* Tome II. *L'Histoire.* Tome III. *Les Civilisations.* Paris: Larose, 1912. Reprint. Paris: G.-P. Maisonneuve et Larose, 1972.

de Zeltner, R.P. Le culte du Nama au Soudan. *Bulletin et Memoires de la Société d'Anthropologie de Paris* 1910; 1:361–362.

Diallo, Yaya and Hall, Mitchell. *The Healing Drum. African Wisdom Teachings.* Rochester, VT: Destiny Books, 1989.

Dieterlen, Germaine. *Essai sur la religion Bambara.* Paris: Presses Universitaires de France, 1951.

———. La Serrure et sa clef (Dogon, Mali). In *Echanges et Communications. Mélanges Offert à Claude Levi-Straus,* edited by J. Poullon and P. Marasse. Paris, The Hague: Mouton, 1970, Volume 1, 7–27.

——— and Cissé, Youssouf. *Les Fondements de la société d'initiation du Komo.* Paris: Mouton & Co., 1970.

Djata, Sundiata A. *The Bamana Empire by the Niger. Kingdom, Jihad and Colonization, 1712–1920.* Princeton, NJ: Markus Wiener Publishers, 1997.

Duthoy, Pascal. Gesculpteerde deursloten bij de Bamana en de Dogon. *Vereniging Vrienden Van Ethnografica* 1999; 66:46–51.

Echenberg, Myron. *Colonial Conscripts. The Tirailleurs Sénégalais in French West Africa, 1957–1960.* London: J. Currey, 1991.

Ezra, Kate. *Art of the Dogon. Selections from the Lester Wunderman Collection.* New York: The Metropolitan Museum of Art/Harry N. Abrams, Inc., 1988.

———. *A Human Ideal in African Art. Bamana Figurative Sculpture.* Washington, DC: Smithsonian Institution Press, 1986.

Frank, Barbara E. *Mande Potters and Leather-Workers. Art and Heritage in West Africa.* Washington, DC and London: Smithsonian Institution Press, 1998.

Fraser, Douglas. *African Art as Philosophy.* New York: Interbook, 1974.

Goldwater, Robert. *Bambara Sculpture from the Western Sudan.* New York: University Publishers, Inc., 1960.

Griaule, Marcel. Réflexions sur les symboles Soudanais. *Cahiers Internationaux de Sociologie* 1952, 13:8–30.

——— and Dieterlen, Germaine. *Signs graphiques Soudanais.* Paris: Hermann et Cie., 1951.

Guariglia, G. *L'Arte dell'Africa Nera e il Suo Messagio.* Parma: Edizione Ismes, 1966.

Harmon, Stephen Albert. *The Expansion of Islam among the Bambara under French Rule: 1890–1940.* Ph.D. dissertation. Ann Arbor, MI: University Microfilms International, 1993.

Henry, Joseph. *L'Ame d'un peuple africain. Les Bambara; leur vie psychique, ethique, sociale, religieuse.* Munster: Aschendorffschen Buchhandlung, 1910 (republished as *L'Ame d'un peuple africain. Les Bambara.* Paris: Picard, 1920).

Imperato, Pascal James. *African Folk Medicine. Practices and Beliefs of the Bambara and Other Peoples.* Baltimore: York Press, 1977.

———. *Buffoons, Queens and Wooden Horsemen. The Dyo and Gouan Societies of the Bambara of Mali.* New York: Kilima House Publishers, 1983.

———. *The Cultural Heritage of Africa.* Chanute, Kansas: Safari Museum Press, 1974.

———. The Dance of the Tyi Wara. *African Arts* 1970, IV(1):8–13, 71–80.

———. The Depiction of Beautiful Women in Malian Youth Association Masquerades. *African Arts* 1994, XXVII (1):58–65, 95.

———. *Dogon Cliff Dwellers. The Art of Mali's Mountain People.* New York: L. Kahan Gallery Inc./African Arts, 1978.

———. Dogon Door Locks. *African Arts* 1978, XI(4):54–57, 96.

———. Door Locks of the Bamana of Mali. *African Arts* 1972, VI(3):52–56, 84.

BIBLIOGRAPHY

————. *Historical Dictionary of Mali.* Third Edition. Lanham, Maryland: The Scarecrow Press, Inc., 1996.

————. *Mali: A Search for Direction.* Boulder, CO : Westview Press, 1989.

————. The Role of Women in Traditional Healing among the Bambara of Mali. *Transactions of the Royal Society of Tropical Medicine and Hygiene 1981*, 75(6):766–770.

————. West African Door Locks. Tribal Arts Gallery Two, New York, June 1974. *African Arts* 1974, VIII(1):68.

————. *A Wind in Africa. A Story of Modern Medicine in Mali.* St. Louis, MO: Warren H. Green, Inc., 1975.

————. The Yayoroba Puppet Tradition of Mali. *The Puppetry Journal* 1981, 32(4):20–26.

————. and Shamir, Marli. Bokolanfini. Mud Cloth of the Bamana of Mali. *African Arts* 1970, III(4):32–41, 80.

Jespers, Philippe. Mask and Utterance: The Analysis of an "Auditory" Mask in the Initiatory Society of the Komo Minyanka, Mali. In *Objects. Signs of Africa.* Edited by Luc de Heusch. Ghent: Snoeck-Ducaju & Zoon, 1996, 37–56.

Jonckers, Danielle. *La Société Minyanka du Mali. Traditions communautaires et développement cotonnier.* Paris: Editions L'Harmattan, 1987.

Kaba, Lansiné. *The Wahhabiyaya. Islamic Reform and Politics in French West Africa.* Evanston, IL: Northwestern University Press, 1974.

Koné, Kassim. *Mande Zana ni Ntalen Wa ni ko. Bamanankan ni Angilekan na.* West Newbury, MA: Mother Tongue Editions, 1995.

Labouret, Henri. *Les Manding et leur langue.* Paris: Librairie Larose, 1934.

Laude, Jean. *African Art of the Dogon. The Myths of the Cliff Dwellers.* New York: The Brooklyn Museum in association with The Viking Press, Inc., 1973.

Lem, F.H. Les Cultes des arbres et de génies protecteurs du sol au Soudan Français. *Bulletin de l'IFAN* 1948, 10:539–559.

Ligers, Z. *Les Sorko (Bozo). Maîtres du Niger. Etude ethno-graphique.* Paris: Librairie des cinq continents, 1964 (Volume I), 1966 (Volume II), 1967 (Volume III), 1969 (Volume IV).

McNaughton, Patrick R. Bamana Blacksmiths. *African Arts* 1979, XII(2):65–71, 92.

————. *Iron Art of the Blacksmith in the Western Sudan.* Lafayette, IN: Purdue University, 1975.

————. *The Mande Blacksmiths. Knowledge, Power, and Art in West Africa.* Bloomington and Indianapolis: Indiana University Press, 1988.

————. *Secret Sculptures of Komo. Art and Power in Bamana (Bambara) Initiation Societies.* Philadelphia: Institute for the Study of Human Issues, 1979.

————. The Shirts That Mande Hunters Wear. *African Arts* 1982, XV(3):54–58, 91.

Molin, Msgr. *Dictionnaire Bambara-Français et Français-Bambara.* Issy-les-Moulineaux: Les Presses Missionaires, 1955.

Monteil, Charles. *Les Bambara de Ségou et du Kaarta. Etude historique, ethnographique et littéraire d'une peuplade du Soudan Français.* Paris: G.P. Maisonneuve & Larose, 1924.

————. *Contes Soudanais.* Paris: Ernest Leroux Editeur, 1905.

N'Diayé, Bokar. *Groupes ethniques au Mali.* Bamako: Editions Populaires, 1970.

Paques, Viviana. *Les Bambara.* Paris: Presses Universitaires de France, 1954.

————. Bouffons sacrés du cercle de Bougouni (Soudan Français). *Journal de la Société des Africanistes* 1954, 24:63–110.

————. Les Samaké. *Bulletin de l'IFAN* 1956, B, 18:369–390.

Pitt-Rivers, Augustus Henry Lane-Fox. *On the Development and Distribution of Primitive Locks and Keys.* London: Chatto and Windus, 1883.

Rain, David. *Eaters of the Dry Season. Circular Labor Migration in the West African Sahel.* Boulder, CO: Westview Press, 1999.

Robbins, Warren M. and Nooter, Nancy Ingraham. *African Art in American Collections.* Washington, DC and London: Smithsonian Institution Press, 1989.

Roberts, Richard. *Warriors, Merchants, and Slaves. The State and the Economy in the Middle Niger Valley, 1700–1914.* Stanford, California: Stanford University Press, 1987.

Rodriques, Georges D. *A Collection of West African Doors and Locks.* New York: Arte Primitivo Inc., 1968.

Rouamba, Amadou. *Les guérisseurs de la forêt sacrée. Croyances et rites thérapeutiques Bambara dans le Bélédougou au Mali.* Paris: Ecole des Hautes Etudes en Sciences Sociales, 1985 (mimeographed doctoral dissertation).

Rovine, Victoria. *Bogolanfini* in Bamako. The Biography of a Malian Textile. *African Arts* 1997, XXX(1):40–51, 94–96.

Segy, Ladislas. *African Sculpture Speaks, Third Edition*, New York: Hill and Wang, 1969.

Silla, Eric. *People Are Not the Same. Leprosy and Identity in Twentieth-Century Mali.* Portsmouth, NH: Heinemann, 1998.

Suys, Bart. Sculptural versierde deuren en deursloten bij de Dogon, de Bambara, en de Senufo (West Afrika). Licenciate thesis. Ghent: Rijksuniversiteit Gent, 1983.

Tauxier, Louis. *Histoire des Bambara.* Paris: Librairie Orientaliste Paul Geuthner, 1942.

———. *La Religion Bambara.* Paris: Librairie Orientaliste Paul Geuthner, 1927.

Tesi, Paule. *Introduction à l'étude des serrures Bambara. Memoire de maîtrise.* Paris, 1972 (microfiche).

Travélé, Moussa. Le Komo ou Koma. *Outre-Mer* 1929, 1:127–150.

———. *Petit Dictionnaire Français-Bambara et Bambara-Français.* Paris: Librairie Orientaliste Paul Geuthner, 1913.

———. *Proverbes et contes Bambara accompagnés d'une traduction Française et précédés d'un abrégé de droit coutumier Bambara et Malinké.* Paris: Librairie Orientaliste Paul Geuthner, 1923.

von Luschan, Felix. Uber Schlösser mit Fullriegeln. *Zeitschrift für Ethnologie* 1916; 48:406–429.

Wâ Kamissoko. *L'Empire du Mali: Un récit de Wâ Kamissoko de Krina enregistré, transcrit, traduit et annoté par Yousouf Tata Cissé.* Paris: Fondation SCOA pour la Promotion de la Recherche Scientifique en Afrique Noire, 1975 (Parts I–III), 1978 (Parts IV–V).

Webb, James L.A., Jr. *Desert Frontier. Ecological and Economic Change along the Western Sahel, 1600–1850.* Madison: University of Wisconsin Press, 1994.

Wooten, Stephen R. Antelope Headdresses and Champion Farmers. Negotiating Meaning and Identity through the Bamana *Ciwara* Complex. *African Arts* 2000, XXXIII(2):18–33, 89–90.

Zahan, Dominique. *Antilopes du soleil. Arts et rites agraires d'Afrique noire.* Vienna: Edition A. Schendl, 1980.

———. *The Bambara.* Leiden: E.J. Brill, 1974.

———. *La Dialectique du verb chez les Bambara.* Paris: Mouton & Co., 1963.

———. Pictographic writing in the Western Sudan. *Man* 1950, 50, 136–138.

———. *Sociétés d'initiation Bambara. Le N'Domo. Le Korè.* Paris: Mouton & Co., 1960.

93

BIBLIOGRAPHY

PASCAL JAMES IMPERATO is a distinguished Africanist and an internationally respected scholar of the history and art of the peoples of Mali. He first traveled to Mali to direct mass immunization programs for the U.S. Public Health Service and the U.S. Agency for International Development. He worked in Mali for five years and then returned several times to assist the Malians with development and medical projects. A leading authority on the art of the Bamana and Dogon peoples of Mali, he is the author of *Dogon Cliff Dwellers. The Art of Mali's Mountain People* (1978), *Buffoons, Queens and Wooden Horsemen. The Dyo and Gouan Societies of the Bambara of Mali* (1983), and *Historical Dictionary of Mali*, Third Edition (1996). Dr. Imperato is currently Distinguished Service Professor and Chair of the Department of Preventive Medicine and Community Health at the State University of New York, Downstate Medical Center.